"In the several d   ;aret I found
out that leaders   Having the
appropriate mor   ve business
direction is   clearly
demonstrates these leadership ideals."

-Bill Matthews, Former VP of Sales, 3M Industrial

"Margaret is an excellent role model that students at St Kate's look up to and respect for her professionalism, her insights and most importantly, her genuine desire to mentor and help young women realize their full potential in their careers.

As an adjunct professor and The Women's Sales Leaders Cohort facilitator, she has shaped the lives of people that she has coached and worked with."

-Mary Jacobs, MA, Director of Center for Sales Innovation,
St Catherine University

"Margaret uses her background and training in leadership to illuminate and bring out your very best traits and skills to lead. Whether you are new or seasoned in a leadership role, she will equip you to be more effective, confident, and to rally and lead your team to success."

-Teresa Thomas, Director, MN Women In Networking (WIN)

"I've always known Margaret as an amazing sales leader, effective with customers, and someone who drives her sales team to be the best of the best. The 10-Minute Leadership Challenge is a must-have for all aspiring and well-established leaders, based off of her tremendous personal experience. It brings forward many ideas that reflect the success that Margaret created in her teams."

-A. Dreis, Channel Operations Manager, 3M Center

"This is a must-read book written by leadership expert, Margaret Smith. It is an excellent investment in your professional development."

-Mary H., Sales and Management University Professor

"The Ten-Minute Leadership Challenge is a book every manager should have. Margaret offers insight on how to identify your strengths and the strengths of your employees, for the success of your business."

-Kim Barnhart, Chair of Houses of Hospitality Supervisory Council

The 10-Minute Leadership CHALLENGE

Margaret Smith

First Edition.

Copyright © 2013 by Margaret Smith

ISBN-13: 978–1483976914

ISBN-10: 1483976912

Cover Design by Jordan Reasor

Acknowledgments

This book is 30 years in the making, so it is difficult to acknowledge all the people who impacted me, taught me valuable lessons, acted as mentors (whether they knew it or not), and in some way contributed to my journey.   So, to all of those people who I worked with, worked for, and who worked for me, thank you. You gave me great stories to pull from, amazing experiences that shaped me as a leader, and challenged me to bring my best self forward, no matter what.

The actual writing, formatting and encouragement to keep going when I got weary of research and typing go to McKenzie Malanaphy and Kate Leibfried. They asked me questions, listened, and wrote as I talked and helped me make sense of my rambling monologues.   They were patient, persistent, and encouraging. Their young minds also helped me realize that my story was one that would help others be better leaders—my ultimate goal.

A big thank you to WiseInk, and especially Dara Beevas, for the support, advice, and professional eye.

I'd be remiss if I did not thank my family. If it was not for their support throughout my career, I would have far fewer stories to share and rich experiences to draw upon. To them, thank you.

Dedication

This book is dedicated to all the leaders still on the journey to be their best and make the difference they are capable of achieving.

All you need is 10 minutes...

The 10-Minute Leadership CHALLENGE

Margaret Smith

Table of Contents

Introduction
What's the Big Idea?

Throughout our lives we are faced with decisions:

> Go here – Go there
> Do this – Do that
> Buy this – Give that away
> No – Yes – Maybe
> Be this – Be that

Each decision requires us to consider our options and the possible consequences, impact, and benefits of those decisions. And then there are the life changes that cause us to look at everything differently. There are the obvious life changes—taking that first step, going to school, getting handed the keys to the family car, moving out, getting married, starting a family, losing someone important in our lives, and on and on.

However, one of the most important life changes is one that is much more subtle. This is moment when we first realize that what we do and say can make a powerful impression on another person. When we realize that others are affected by our words, our attitude, and our actions, we truly become part of the world in a new way. We become more conscious of who we are *and* mindful of the people we encounter on our journey.

As leaders, we are expected to be self-aware and awake at the wheel.

Leaders are also expected to deal with the curve balls life tends to throw at us. I've been thrown a few that challenged me and left bruises (you probably have too!). It's what we do to heal, what we learn from the experience, and how we use it to help others that matters.

I have had amazing experiences during my business career. I've worked for wonderful, generous, value-driven, ethical, caring companies. It wasn't the "company" that embodied all those descriptors, it was the people within the company.

I worked for leaders that challenged me to be the best I could be, saw talent in me that I did not see in myself, offered me opportunities to demonstrate those skills, and opened doors that I never expected to be available to me. There were also people that stepped in my way, cut me off, and held me back. I learned from all of those experiences. They are the fodder that helped define and shape me as a business leader.

When I decided to retire in 2009, I took a step back and reflected on my amazing journey. I thought about the incredible responsibilities I had been given, the places I visited, the people I met, the relationships I developed, and the businesses I grew, sold, and bought. As I reflected, I began to feel a strong desire, even a commitment to give back. I had learned many professional skills and practices during my time in management, and there were numerous ways I could assist ambitious business leaders: I could help shorten the career ladder for someone else; I could help an aspiring manager develop into a better leader; I could enable a greater level of satisfaction and engagement in an organization; I could get a team to hum...

So, I began coaching mid-level managers, teams, and leadership boards at all stages in their careers. I began to dissipate my leadership development knowledge through lectures and seminars. I even walked right over to a local university and asked, "How can I help?" Teaching undergraduate level business classes is a thrill I never expected and gives me the opportunity to encourage, excite, and ignite a spark in those just entering their careers.

This journey led me to read, research, observe, and create the list of leadership skills in the ten chapters you will read in this book. My hope is that this book will allow me to expand my reach and touch the lives of aspiring businessmen and women who are looking for a little guidance on their career journey. Today is the day to start honing your skills and striving to be your best self. **Take the challenge.**

How to Use
This Book

I came up with the idea of ten minute chapters when I reflected on how much time we have in our busy schedules and how long it takes to **be inspired, grab hold of an idea, think of one or two action items, and make a plan.** I also did not want a heavy, theoretical, deeply strategic book, but one that was practical, simple, and realistic.

Each chapter should take ten minutes to read. The basic sections in each are:

- My story, real life experiences, and what I learned
- Content and action items
- Your arsenal (ideas for an action plan)
- A place for your notes, ideas, and insights

There are ten chapters in this book. I initially thought of writing twelve chapters (one for each month of the year), but then I realized that we all need a break, vacation, or breather every once and a while. I decided to go with ten chapters, to allow for a couple of one-month breaks during the year. Give yourself thirty days to implement your action plan: try something new, observe, read, adjust, and try again. Then move onto the next skill.

Have fun and give yourself a ten minute gift. The people you lead, the organization you work for, and the clients you serve will appreciate it too!

1. Authenticity

DARE to be yourself.

> **"The privilege of a lifetime is to become who you truly are."**
>
> -C.G. Jung

My Story

Authenticity is a hot topic these days. Employees have a genuine yearning for authentic leadership and role models. They want leaders who are true to themselves and who put forward their genuine personas in both their personal lives and their careers. Authentic leaders are reliable, trustworthy, and highly valuable in the business world.

When I ponder authentic behavior and identity, I often think of an Executive Vice President I met after I moved to Saint Paul, Minnesota from my sales position on the east coast. We were both marketing supervisors and got to know each other because of the close proximity of our cubicles. As we both climbed the career ladder and he ultimately became an Executive Vice President, he continued to keep an open office and encouraged employees at all levels to come directly to him with any issues they might be facing. He genuinely valued human relationships and did not let his prestigious position interfere with the friendships he had made in the lower levels of the company.

Whenever I passed him in the hall, he was quick to wave hello and spend a few minutes chatting and catching up. He behaved exactly the way he always had—friendly and communicative, open and approachable. He interacted with me as if we were still marketing supervisors, chatting between our cubicles.

It is because of this authenticity that I was able to approach this individual time and again when I was confronting issues or simply needed to hash out a dilemma. When I would walk through the door of his office, he would not act annoyed or superior or make me feel small. Instead, he would greet me with a friendly smile, ask about my family, and then talk to me as an equal. One time when I visited his office I remember him saying, "Margaret, great to see you again. I'm so glad you stopped by my office; I feel like I always learn something from you."

He meant what he said, pure and simple. He genuinely cared about my input and my contribution to the company and let me know it. When I think about authenticity in my own life—whether personal or business—I think about this particular E.V.P. and do my best to emulate his example. No matter how high you rise, it is important to keep your feet on the ground and your body in its own skin. It starts with knowing who you are.

Self-Awareness

Self-aware people are perceptive people. They have a strong sense of who they are and how others see them. They are adept at interacting with others, paying attention to their own words and actions as well as the words and actions of those around them. Take the time to slow down and think about your role in the work place. How do others perceive you? How do you see yourself? How do you fit in with your co-workers? If you are a person whose mind is always going a mile a minute, it is especially important to take a breath, stop multi-tasking, and simply pay attention to yourself, your co-workers, and your interactions with others. This level of awareness is important. If you don't have a solid idea of how you impact people, how are you going to motivate and inspire them?

Keep in mind that it is normal and natural to modify your behavior in different situations. Certain circumstances might call for a more quiet, reserved version of you while other circumstances might call for an assertive, boisterous version of you. Along the same lines, you may have to interact with some people differently than others. For instance, you would probably adjust your style of storytelling when interacting with someone who prefers to get to the point quickly, whereas you might really dig into the details of a great story when interacting with someone who thrives on the conversation and loves hearing every piece of your experience. You might change your language, your level of formality, even your posture in different situations. However, even though you are modifying your behavior, you are not changing the essential you. You can tweak your style of interaction without losing yourself in the shuffle.

> "There's the **you** you are, the **you** you think you are, the **you** others think you are, and the **you** you think others think you are."
>
> -Unknown

In my current work as a career coach, clients sometimes ask me to help them overcome a professional relationship challenge they are facing—one that is hampering their career. As we work together on strategies and develop potential steps to try, they invariably ask about being authentic. "If I modify my approach, am I being someone I am not? Am I being inauthentic?" The truth is NO, not as long as you have a deep understanding of who you are at your very core. I tell these clients that they shouldn't be afraid to challenge the status quo or ask tough questions, as long as they do it in a way that supports and substantiates their true selves.

Bridges That Last

As a leader, it is important to let your true self shine through. By letting others see the real you, you are opening yourself up to genuine interactions and candid conversations. Co-workers value this authenticity. They appreciate the fact that they know exactly who they are working with and that there will be no big surprises when a deadline or an important meeting rolls around. **This is the kind of consistency that lets others trust you and feel comfortable enough around you to share their hopes, trepidations, and ideas.**

As a manager, I did my best to gain others' trust by putting forth my genuine persona *and* by encouraging open dialogue. There were times I felt as though I had one of those neon "OPEN" signs hanging outside of my office door. My approachable, supportive, and inquisitive nature was well-known. It encouraged co-workers to come to me for brain-storming, problem solving, or just a listening ear.

One of those open dialogues led to a wonderful new business opportunity and an innovative product development project. It began when a business development marketer walked into my office and shared an idea a customer of his had. The customer asked if we would help develop a product solution. He had been turned down once before, but really believed in the idea. Together, we hashed out the questions he should ask, the research he needed to do, and the business case required to gain support. He walked out of my office with new energy, excitement, and commitment to the project and began to work on its implementation. I checked recently and the business that marketer started is now worth well over $10 million and growing. Amazing things can happen when you approach each person with your true, authentic self—you create trust, encourage open dialogue, and hopefully begin to challenge each other in a positive way.

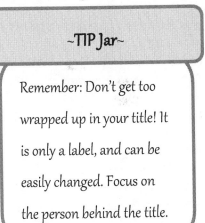

~TIP Jar~

Remember: Don't get too wrapped up in your title! It is only a label, and can be easily changed. Focus on the person behind the title.

It shouldn't matter whether you move up the ladder, change roles, or even change companies. **The relationships you build with others should be consistent, genuine, and natural**.

We all engage with people in our lives differently. Some of us are extremely social and glean strength from human interactions while others prefer keeping interactions to a minimum. No one says you have to spend long periods of time chatting with your co-workers over coffee and bagels. If that's not you, then it's simply not you (in contrast, if that *is* you, bring on the bagels!). Figure out what style of interaction works for you and go for it. If you are all about short, five-minute exchanges, then become a master of concise conversations. If you prefer interacting with groups of co-workers, then make an effort to do so.

Remember, establishing bonds and building trust amongst co-workers takes time and you want to do it right. Stick to the style that best suits you and the people around you will soon feel comfortable with your method of communication. No surprises. No swings. Just you, interacting with them, in a genuine way.

Authenticity = Sustainability

How does a business retain its employees? Maybe salary and benefits have something to do with it. But in the end, the true things that make a person want to stick with a company are a strong sense of belonging and the feeling that their authentic self is valued. A good leader fosters an atmosphere of mutual trust and dependability. They put forth their authentic self, create genuine relationships with their employees, and expect the same kind of authenticity in return.

By building a workplace network based on trust and compassion, a good leader is better able to retain his or her staff and better equipped to weather any storms the company might face.

Getting to know your employees and co-workers for their strengths and unique talents allows you to pick the right people for a project, know whom you can go to for what activity, and bring out the best in everyone.

Ever feel like a square peg in a round hole? This happens when someone asks you to do something but did not take the time to really consider if you're the best person for the job. They did not spend enough time evaluating others' strengths to determine who might rise to the occasion, who has the skills and talents required, or who needs a new twist and would thrive in the role. By really getting to know the attributes and aspirations of the people around you the "machine becomes well oiled," the quality and timeliness of projects increases, and people are smiling and thriving. Sounds like a fun and satisfying work environment to me!

Know Your Flaws

Ok. You know the value of being authentic. You understand the importance of building inter-office relationships based on trust and mutual dependability, but what about the side of you that you'd rather not show others? Those features are a part of you as well and, like it or not, if you're creating an open atmosphere around yourself, they *will* show through. But don't stress too much. **A large part of being your authentic self is knowing your weaknesses and recognizing where you can improve**. You're not perfect. No one is. But you can modify your core self to be a better, healthier, more well-rounded version of you.

A big step towards correcting any bothersome character flaws you might have is simply recognizing them (tying back to our earlier discussion about self-awareness). People who are self-aware are perceptive enough to recognize both their strengths and weaknesses. We are trained to spend time looking at our strengths, but human nature plays tricks on us when it comes to weaknesses. We cannot always see them. It is healthy to be aware of both—an assessment, formal performance appraisal, or even a casual conversation with a close colleague or friend can help you better understand what you do well and what areas could use improvement.

I concur with the work of Tom Rath, author of "Strengths-finders." He believes we should be aware of our weaknesses and look for those things that have been called out more than once. Is something you do holding you back and causing you to stumble? Then do something about it. With a little focus and mindfulness, you should be able to get to the heart of your issues and begin solving them. But don't spend the majority of your time here.

If you find yourself floundering and can't quite pinpoint the cause(s) of your troubles, don't be afraid to ask! You have a network of people around you who know you and care. Your friends and family want to see you succeed and will most likely be eager to help in any way they can. Just be sure to make it clear you *want* constructive criticism and _will not_ get defensive when they offer their opinions. Sometimes it is tough to hear others vocalize their thoughts about how we might improve ourselves. Keep in mind that these people are guides. They are coaches. Just like a basketball player or a violinist needs an instructor to criticize, offer advice, and push them to do better, so too do business professionals need constructive guidance and practice.

Study your strengths. How can you make them even more obvious? What actions demonstrate those strengths? Once you have a good idea of how to capitalize on your strengths, take action to make them better.

<u>And don't forget to listen</u>. Reflect. Figure out what you can and should do in order to be your authentic self. Then act.

Remember: your authentic self is great! Even though you probably have some areas you would like to improve upon, have the courage to be a little vulnerable and share yourself with others. Feeling comfortable in your skin, exposing your genuine self, and building authentic relationships is all part of becoming a great leader.

Your arsenal

☑ Think about your role within the office. Is this the role you'd like to play? If so, are you giving it your all? If not, how can you work towards your dream role?

☑ Take an assessment that helps you identify your strengths and builds your self-awareness.

☑ Slow down and take the time to reflect on your personal traits. Whatever you do well, do it better!

☑ Make a self-understanding plan. Think about what is impeding your success and jot down some ideas on how you can change and improve. Who may help?

☑ Work towards creating open lines of communication with your co-workers. What can you do to be more approachable?

☑ Be aware of how people react to you, your comments, or observations. Their behavior can tell you a lot about your own personality or tendencies.

Notes

_____

_____

_____

_____

_____

_____

_____

_____

_____

_____

_____

_____

_____

_____

_____

_____

_____

_____

_____

2. Courage
Stand Up; Stand Tall

> **"What would life be if we had not courage to attempt anything?"**
> -Vincent Van Gogh

My Story

In the late '90s, I was running a business within my division. One of the product lines was struggling due to the current demands of the market. Although the product was innovative and functional, it became impractical to continue investing in it. After careful consideration and analysis, a decision was made to sell this branch of the business.

I compiled a team to put together a sales package and we went through the due diligence of marketing the business to potential buyers. During this time, I was surprised to learn that my team was increasingly convinced we should not sell. They believed we could turn it around. My team asked me if I would meet with the vice president and persuade him to reevaluate the decision.

At this point, I had the choice to do one of two things: I could play it safe, remain within my boundaries of comfort, and say, "No. He approved the sale of this business, and we're going to follow through." Or, I could take a courageous leap and follow through with my team's wishes. I chose the latter, and asked my team to compile an effective, clear, and believable business case for keeping the business that could be communicated confidently.

I went to the V.P.'s office with my prepared argument and the package my team had worked hard to put together. Despite my team's efforts and all of our research, the original decision could not be changed.

However, our inability to change the decision did not mean that my course of action had been an outright failure. Approaching the vice president allowed me to gain a better understanding of the decision to sell the business. During our discussion, he shared a more in-depth explanation of the vision for the use of the resources that would be freed up through this divestiture. Although, officially, I left the room defeated, I also left the room with a much better understanding of the business case and strategy behind the decision.

Back with my team, I explained what had happened and relayed what I learned. Sharing the information allowed everyone to have a more thorough understanding of how this divestiture enabled future opportunities for everyone.

Whether we went through with the sale or not, the choice to present our case to the vice president benefitted my team and me. Not only did the additional knowledge help us with the sale, but having more input caused less foot-dragging during the process. This meant less time wasted and a genuine interest in the endeavor. The experience was also a lesson for me.

I was now aware of how necessary it is to gain clarity right off the bat. Asking a lot of questions from the get-go, even if it's uncomfortable or intimidating, would have allowed me to give my organization the bigger picture from the start. Through my decision to present my team's case, we were able to share a communal vision of the bigger and brighter future of our company.

Meeting with my V.P. one-on-one also changed our relationship for the better. He was more approachable than I thought he would be and, because of my professional courage, his opinion of me as a business leader was enhanced. Superiors do not, of course, want each and every one of their decisions to be challenged. But, in my case, the action allowed my boss to see me in the role of someone with the confidence to challenge business decisions and practices in a constructive way: with preparation and respect.

What is Courage?

The word courage can elicit a variety of images. From the bravery of men and women going into battle to the courage to stand up for yourself, your values, or the people around you, courage takes on many different forms in our daily lives. Perhaps we decide to try something new or perform a routine task in an out-of-the-ordinary way. Maybe we finally work up the courage to ask our boss out for lunch, enter a room full of strangers to give a presentation, or manage a dramatic and unpredicted change. The initial courageous leap is only the beginning. You have to be ready to go two-hundred miles an hour at the drop of a hat, because once you've taken that risk, things can often become fast-paced and intense.

Often, we demonstrate courage naturally, taking a deep breath and calmly moving forward, or thinking on our feet and reacting spontaneously to the situation at hand. Beyond the initial courage to act and the quick change of pace, **courage also concerns the way we handle ourselves in all stages of a tough situation**. How will you weather the storm that will likely develop? Did you manage with synergy, support, and excitement, or did you fall prey to dissention, disorganization, and cynicism?

In today's business environment, courage is more crucial than ever. Our workplaces are rapidly changing and hyper-competitive. Because of this atmosphere, we can be tempted to waiver and just do what we're told or back down from voicing our opinions and taking risks. **Courage, faith, and confidence are intertwined**.

> "Inaction breeds doubt and fear. Action breeds confidence and courage. If you want to conquer fear, do not sit home and think about it. Go out and get busy." -Dale Carnegie

Do you believe strongly enough in your intuition and ability to make a sound decision? Are you willing to work hard to prove you're right? Do you have the courage to get into that driver's seat and be the best version of yourself, despite the fact that there will always be room for error and significant risk?

When making a courageous decision or change, it is paramount that you have faith in yourself and your team. Take the time to prepare a plan to succeed. When facing a courageous change, consider whether or not you've taken advantage of all the lifelines around you. Have you made use of the many sources of knowledge and support in your workplace? Have you given significant thought to the details that could undermine your plan? All of these questions—and all of this research and preparation—is key to your success.

Eventually, you get in the driver's seat and you're off! Enjoy the ride and always remember to pay attention to what your colleagues, partners, and competitors around you are doing. There is usually an opportunity or two to learn from the techniques and experiences of others. While on the road, ask yourself, "Who are the experts I want to contact for advice? And who are the people that would only impede my mission?"

Once you've decided to take courageous action, remember to carry yourself in a professional and consistent manner. Maintain a "confident calm" in order to be effective and win the respect and faith of others.

As a leader, people intently watch your reactions to situations. Because of this, the whole organization often adopts and reflects the character of its leader. If the leader believes, the group will believe. If a leader expresses concerns or reservations about a particular direction, or doubt concerning whether or not their team is capable of completing a particular project, the team is going to be in a state of reservation, stress, and potential paranoia.

No matter how well-prepared you are for a courageous action, there is always the potential that you'll be derailed. People might ask you tough questions, attempt to take the reins of the conversation, or completely dismiss your ideas. These things happen; do not let them ruffle your feathers. Maintain your confident calm and answer questions or challenges as best you can. And if you don't know an answer or haven't thought about a particular aspect of your plan, be honest! People can see right through hesitation and waffling. Instead, say, "Good question, that's an area we have not explored in detail. I'll do some additional research and get back to you. But what I do know is this..." Then, get back on track and continue where you left off.

Remember, the better informed you are before you go into a meeting, the less likely you'll be thrown for a loop. Take the time to focus on the main points of your plan (without wasting valuable

~TIP Jar~

When Confidence is Flagging:

1. Buy time: repeat back questions before answering.

2. Don't make statements you can't back up.

3. Don't panic: breathe slowly and deeply, square your shoulders, and speak steadily.

time and energy on the minute, nit-picky details) and anticipate questions others might have.

But what if your meeting goes downhill quickly? What happens if your boss or the committee are unimpressed or unenthusiastic about your idea/plan/proposal? **Take it in stride**. At the very least, you've demonstrated to your co-workers that you are willing to stand up for an idea or action that you believe in and take the courageous leap to present it to others. **Make sure you to learn from your setbacks, rather than dwell on them**. Every experience like this is a learning experience, a "shaping moment."

Don't focus on the fact that you didn't win the race. Instead, redirect your focus to the fact that you finished the race. Remember that failure does not negate the many things that went right. Celebrate your successes and move on. You have important work to do and there is no use moping about your setbacks!

Additionally, demonstrate your continued support for your company. If they do not accept the changes you've proposed, don't get bitter or argumentative. Instead, try to understand why they are choosing a specific course of action and support them as best you can (without compromising your values, of course).

The courage my team exemplified during the sale of the declining business made me a more desirable employee. My boss recognized me as a proactive leader. It also changed the relationship I had with my team for the better.

You might think that failure would have resulted in my team seeing me as someone who was incapable of relaying their proposal. This was not the case. Some of these people had spent their entire careers working on this business we had been asked to sell. These team members were real stakeholders in the work we did. Because I was open to their opinions and had the courage to relay their message, my team saw me as a leader who was willing to stand up for them. I took a *risk* for *them* and they appreciated and respected my efforts. Most importantly, my team had a renewed confidence in their ability to approach me with their opinions and ideas.

The shared "failure" of our proposal made my team closer, created openness between us, and allowed the team to trust my leadership. They had confidence that I respected their opinions and the commitment that they had to the business. They felt appreciated, not just cast aside.

Courage Builds Community

When you demonstrate a willingness to take risks, other risk-takers and people with new and out-of-the-box ideas will be drawn to you. This is because you appear comfortable with the idea of change and are thereby a viable source of consultation, advice, and support for people. For me, this means that when someone else has a good idea, I want others to say, "go see Margaret, she's not afraid of anything." People want to approach you because they know that you aren't opposed to pushing the envelope. This encourages the group to think creatively, improve the status quo, and tackle tough problems. A company's greatest resource is its people; the more comfortable your employees are in approaching you and one another, the more productive and forward-thinking your business will be.

Courage Catapults Careers

Another example of my personal experience with professional courage was my decision to take on a new and challenging project in an area previously foreign to my company and me. The change followed a casual conversation with my national sales manager at a trade show. The sales manager and I were talking about how we could redefine the business we were in. We kicked around the idea to create a new services-centered branch for our business to compliment our product-centered business model. The services provided would be some of the first intangible products ever offered by our company. The conversation had been a casual, "what if" conversation that you laugh and joke about, but really don't think of in any concrete terms. However, two weeks later, the vice president of the company walked into my office, and said, "I heard about your idea to create a services-centered branch of the company. I'd like to give it a try *and* I'd like you to take the reins. Come back to me in two weeks, let me know what you need to get started, and what value this will add to the company."

Needless to say, I was a little taken aback. Here I was again, faced with a decision involving professional courage. I could have allowed the new and unknown to intimidate me. I could have explained that I didn't feel as if I was the right person for the job, or I hadn't seriously considered the option and felt unprepared. Instead, I took a leap of courage, had faith in myself and my abilities, and committed to making the change. As a result, my team and I successfully created a new branch of the company revolving entirely around services.

I researched external organizations with similar models outside of our market and met with people from those companies. Through these meetings, I gained the added bonus of getting to know some phenomenal people that shared similar visions and goals. These experiences added depth to my knowledge and perspective. I also had the opportunity to work with many like-minded people within my company; they became good friends and valuable advocates in other business opportunities and challenges I faced. I would have never met these wonderful individuals had I not ventured into new territory and worked with others outside of my usual office bubble.

> "He who is not courageous enough to take risks will accomplish nothing in life."
>
> -Muhammad Ali

This exhilarating and energizing experience took my career to places I never thought it would and instilled in me a fortified conviction in my own abilities and business acumen. If I had turned down the opportunity, perceiving it as too big a risk, I would have missed a fantastic opportunity to develop and test myself. Instead of focusing on the intimidating and negative "what ifs," I focused on the positives of potential self-growth and the success of the company.

Your arsenal

- ☑ Is there a component of your job that is unsatisfactory to you? What steps can you take to improve it? Jot down notes and ideas.

- ☑ Create an action plan to improve one aspect of the workplace. Identify the key players who have the ability to change the status quo and schedule a meeting with them this month.

- ☑ Approach a boss or colleague who has always been intimidating to you OR who you do not know very well. Make an effort to start a conversation with them or ask for their input on a project.

- ☑ Is your routine getting a little too comfortable? Have the courage to shake things up! Have lunch with someone new, take a class, or redecorate your office. It's healthy to get out of your comfort zone every once and a while.

- ☑ At your next meeting, share your opinion. Have the courage to listen to positive as well as critical feedback.

Notes

3. Trust
Earn, Extend, and Enhance

"It is the mutual bond of trust and respect that acts as the catalyst that creates high performance. Not only must you trust others, but even more important, they must trust you."
-Brian Tracy, CEO BTI

My Story

I was leading a sales organization for a part of the country that was heavily populated with traditional businesses—woodworking companies, food and beverage suppliers, metalworking shops, and automotive companies. For decades, these businesses had been my company's long-standing strength. Over time, however, technology, relocation of businesses, and a general reduction in the demand for the products from these industries resulted in a sales decline. All the things we did in the past were not working and our results reflected that. We knew our customers appreciated our product knowledge, quality, and service, and we wanted them to continue to rely on us for their manufacturing needs. So, how could we possibly hit our aggressive sales targets?

My company believed we could sell a wider variety of products to our existing customer base. Additionally, there were probably untapped opportunities to expand sales to an entirely new set of customers. The trick was: how could we *specifically* go about increasing sales to both sets of customers in a cost-effective, timely manner? I laid out the situation to my sales leadership team and asked them to come up with some possible solutions. They knew our sales goals, what stakeholders expected from us, the skills of their teams, the demographics of the markets they served, and the capacity of the organization. Even though the issue was pressing, I left the sales leaders in a conference room to brainstorm solutions. I didn't offer my input; I didn't prescribe any possible answers to our marketing quandary. Instead, I took a leap of faith in my team and trusted their ability to solve our problem.

Three hours later, I returned to the group and was amazed. They had done some basic research, made phone calls, drew up charts, and laid out a plan to accomplish all that was expected of us. There is no way I could have done this on my own; they had the intimate knowledge that cracked the code, so to speak. I asked them to think about what it would take to implement their plan. *Again, I left.* I came back two hours later. My team had created the entire plan, complete with details such as: where we would focus our resources, who would handle particular assignments, what training was needed, and what specific tasks needed to be accomplished. All I had to do was agree with the plan and subsequently gain support from upper management for implementing the changes.

I trusted my team, and they rose to the occasion. I allowed them the freedom to brainstorm, create, and think outside the box without feeling the pressure of management looking over their shoulders. They had room to innovate and make full use of their knowledge and talents. I could have easily approached my team and given them a set of strict parameters. I could have easily micro-managed and laid out the path that *I* felt we should take. Instead, I trusted their abilities and demonstrated complete faith in their capacity to create a set of effective strategies. The result: I was blown away by my sales leaders' plan *and* my team experienced a surge of confidence in themselves and a new respect for my leadership. They appreciated my high level of trust in them and were eager to show me that I hadn't made a mistake.

After the sales leaders shared their plan, we implemented changes in areas that required minimal cost and could be put into practice quickly in order to test their strategies. We monitored the progress of our plan, saw it was working, and proceeded to make more aggressive changes. Within a few months, we saw improvement in sales, higher morale from the organization, and a reestablished belief that we could win. Simply put, I trusted my leadership team to have the answers, and *this* was the source of our success.

Trust in Three Parts

Trust is the foundation of every successful, healthy human relationship. It is also paramount to the success of your career and business. When considering trust, we can break it up into three parts: earning the trust of others, building our trust in others, and maintaining reciprocal trust.

I believe we are born with the propensity to trust. We are not born as pathological liars or skeptics with hate in our hearts and aversion to commitment. The experiences we accrue throughout our lives are what cause us to become fearful. Fear dictates what we're willing to do on a daily basis and dissuades us from taking chances. If the people in your life trust you not to badger them or blame them for a failure, *and* rely on you to listen and offer sound advice, everyone benefits. Look for the good in others and you will find it there. Have faith that, when things take an unexpected turn, you can rely on others to collaborate and troubleshoot.

Keep in mind that trust in a business setting looks a lot like trust in your personal life. We are surrounded by a network of people who often count on us to follow-through with commitments, show up on time, or hold up our end of a deal. It is important to foster trust in our lives because we do not live in a vacuum. Even if your average work day does not consist of team activities, you are NOT alone. You are surrounded by co-workers, clients, friends, bosses, etc. and it is absolutely necessary to learn to work together in harmony. Perhaps at times you will have to make a leap of faith in others and trust that they will get things done by the deadline or do above average work on a project but, **as a leader, people should never feel like <u>they</u> need to take a leap of faith in order to trust <u>you</u>.**

Earning Trust

We all earn trust the same way: through consistent, positive behavior. Your actions are the building blocks of a healthy relationship. When creating trust, consider your tone, your attitude, and the way in which you support the people around you. Consistency in your actions allows others to feel assured because they know what to expect. This does not necessarily mean that they can always predict what your response will be. Instead, people feel certain of the integrity of your course of action and the trusting, respectful point from which you act. Because of this consistency, others feel comfortable coming to you. They know you'll offer support and make time to listen. Consistently demonstrate an open mind and your team will benefit from a more inclusive atmosphere. Earn the trust of others and you'll be challenged to learn, consulted by many, and included in strategic discussions.

One important part of earning trust is focusing on your follow-through. Do you honor your commitments? Do you show up when you say you will? Do you consistently deliver the high-quality work that you promise? If not, it is time to take a step back and ask yourself why you are not the outstanding employee that you'd like to be. Perhaps you are juggling too many projects. Or maybe your poor memory is holding you up (For more on making your projects click, see chapter six, *No Excuses*). Whatever the case may be, it is time to have an honest conversation with yourself and brainstorm solutions. Maybe you need to create a project map with a timeline of milestones. Or maybe you just need to stop wearing so many hats and focus on one or two things that you do best.

Identify what is holding you back from having consistent follow-through and start fixing it today! Trust takes a while to build, so you really don't have time to waste when it comes to laying down a solid foundation, based on consistent actions and follow-through.

But what if you already have stellar follow-through? What if you consistently deliver high-quality products on or before their deadline? Well, that's fantastic. You're off to a great start, but you're not there yet. Concentrating on follow-through and consistency is a great way to boost your credibility, but it may not serve to build relationships between yourself and co-workers on a more personal level. This is the other side of trust: be approachable to co-workers or clients. **No hidden agendas, no two-faced behavior, no saying this and doing that.** Why would people want to share ideas with you if they question your trustworthiness?

Say what you mean and follow through with your commitments. That is the very essence of trust-building.

Extending Trust

Perhaps others trust you, but do you trust them? It is not always easy to place faith in others, especially when it concerns a big project or risky endeavor. If you are a perfectionist, it can be a tremendous leap to place your faith in the work of others. What if they fail? What if they do things differently than how you would have done them? My response: you'll never find out unless you try."But why should I try?" you might ask. "Why should I entrust Susan with a project if I know she might fail? Why should I let Steven take the reins when he hasn't *asked* me to lead our latest project?" Because placing your trust in others leads to a solid business foundation. You are a part of a team and, like it or not, you depend on others for your company's success. This is a hard lesson for some entrepreneurs to learn. Many ambitious business people would like to climb their way to the top of the ladder without assistance, but this is simply not plausible (and even if it were, would you really want to make the journey by yourself?). Look around you. Your company relies on all the bosses, teammates, and understudies who make up its infrastructure. If you do not trust others with important projects or tasks, how can your company perform? It cannot. It will crumble. It is time to pocket a bit of your pride and learn to lean on others just a little.

~TIP Jar~

Effectively Delegate:

-Stop believing you're the only one who can do the job properly.

-Focus on employee growth as well as results

-Check on progress and provide feedback

Part of entrusting your co-workers involves the smart delegation of tasks. As a leader, **you should know the strengths and weakness of those who work directly beneath you**. You should know what gets them excited and what assignments they dread. You should know where they shine. And if you don't? Find out. It is as simple as sitting down with them and asking for feedback about their latest assignment. Do not steer the conversation; rather, ask for honest input and then *listen* to their response. Find out what makes them tick. Once you have gotten to know your employees, it should be easy to delegate suitable assignments for them. But don't forget to challenge them every once and a while. When people stretch out of their comfort zones and try new things, they become well-rounded individuals *and* your company will benefit from having employees with a wide range of skills and a broad knowledge base.

In short, delegate tasks, help your employees grow, and trust that they will do their best. This kind of trust fosters a positive, nurturing environment where individuals will begin to feel needed; they will begin to feel like they are part of something. By giving others a chance to make a significant contribution to your company, you are giving them the opportunity to flourish and thrive in their current role. That is how you build a sense of company pride and develop a loyal and enthusiastic staff.

This kind of grassroots-level focus is part of what makes companies such as DreamWorks successful. All employees—even its accountants and lawyers— who work for the animation giant are encouraged to experiment, try out new ideas, and communicate openly with their higher-ups. When they have an idea, they do not stifle it. Instead, they are encouraged to lay their idea on the table for consideration and are often entrusted to act upon it. According to Dan Satterthwaite, head of DreamWorks' human resources, it's important, "to feel integrated and part of the company, no matter what your job is." He goes on to say, "We challenge all our employees to be their own CEOs." Such impressive employee

> "Trust necessarily carries with it uncertainties, but we must force ourselves to think about these uncertainties as possibilities and opportunities, not as liabilities."
>
> —Robert C. Solomon

engagement is what helped to make DreamWorks one of the "best companies to work for" in 2013.

Extending trust can be difficult, especially if you are a perfectionist, but sometimes you have to let go just a little bit and give others a chance. Sure, they might not perform a task or assignment in the exact way you might do it, but that's ok! Let them try and be ready to coach them through mistakes or hang-ups. Remember that extending trust is just as important as earning it. As a leader, it is your job to manage a team and let each person make whatever contribution they can to that team. Because you can't do everything yourself (and really shouldn't!), have the courage to place an ounce of faith in others.

Cultivate Trust

Cultivating an atmosphere of trust involves creating and maintaining an open, honest environment in the workplace. To maintain trust is to constantly keep yourself in check. Every once and a while take the time to ask yourself, "Are you following through with your commitments? Are you reaching out to others and making an honest effort to learn about them? Are people coming to you when they have a problem or question?" If not, it is time for a little trust upkeep. Cultivating an atmosphere of trust takes constant vigilance. Although it is easy to let things slip between the cracks ("I'll just have a meeting with Robert *next* week" OR "I'm not *that* late for my project deadline), don't. Focus and refocus as often as you need to. And take notes along the way. If you gain some insight about a certain employee, be sure to write it down. Even if you have an excellent memory, it is beneficial to keep notes about your co-workers in a private file or spreadsheet and refer back to them before a one-on-one meeting with that individual. Don't forget to jot down the little things such as their spouse's name, their children's extracurriculars, or the type of dog they own. Even if you are the type of person who likes to get to the point of a meeting and get things done, bringing up a few tidbits of personal information in conversation can help your employee feel more at ease and genuinely cared for.

Another part of cultivating an atmosphere of trust is avoiding micro-management. Let your employees take breaks now and then and do their assignments without you standing over their shoulder. They should feel free to get their work done at their own pace (within the deadline, of course) and by their own methods. Some people work better with a little background music. Others work better when they take a short break every few hours. As long as your team members are not disturbing others' work or missing their deadlines, why should you micro-manage their work style?

Remember, there is a difference between giving your employees space and being too lax. Yes, trust your co-workers—give them freedom, entrust them with assignments—but also be sure to let them know there is a line. You will trust them, but they also have to prove themselves. Don't let yourself be taken advantage of. You can give people second (or third!) chances, but **draw a line somewhere AND let them know exactly where that line is**. During your one-on-one meetings, be sure to set goals, then stick to those goals. If a goal or deadline is not met ask, "What could you have done differently to make this deadline?" Talk about potential solutions and ask what you can do to help your employee meet their goals next time.

When Trust is Tested

But what if you place your trust in someone and they consistently fail to deliver? That can be a blow to your faith in that person and can certainly damage the level of trust you place in them. If someone violates your trust by constantly dropping the ball on projects, showing up late to important meetings, or failing to live up to clients' expectations, don't give up on them right away! If your one-on-one meetings are having little impact AND you honestly believe that person is trying his or her best to succeed, then something else might be going on. Ask yourself, "Is this person a good fit for their position? Am I assigning them appropriate tasks?" And then ask your troubled employee the same questions. Get a dialogue going. It could very well be that this person has been misplaced in your company. Perhaps they are bored or over-whelmed or frustrated with their current role. Consider whether or not this person might thrive in a different position within your organization.

If you have exhausted your options—private meetings, goal-setting, open dialogue, possible re-assignment—and you are still experiencing difficulties with a certain employee, it is time to make a tough decision. If you have to let an employee go, it should not be a surprise to him or her. Your expectations have been clear, you have fostered an open line of communication, and you have placed your trust in the individual and offered them a second or third chance when they failed. At this stage in the game there is nothing left to do. It is time to find someone else who you can trust.

But, keep heart! It is rare to reach this point with an employee, especially if you are putting forth an honest effort to earn trust and extend trust. Most people respond well to a workplace that cultivates the kind of mutual trust we expect from people in our personal lives: our friends, family, teachers, mentors, etc. We are all in this together, so we might as well have a little faith in each other.

Your arsenal

- ☑ Set up one-on-one meetings with employees that you don't know very well. Get to know them a little before discussing business.

- ☑ Give praise: A simple acknowledgement of good work, impressive progress, or a unique path taken keeps others energized and on-task.

- ☑ Practice delegation. Don't be afraid to transfer some responsibility to others' hands.

- ☑ Eliminate distractions: Identify your greatest distractions at work and brainstorm ways to minimize their impact.

- ☑ Take a look at your own work. Do you meet deadlines? Are you completing high-quality work? Would you trust yourself with a project? Jot down some notes on how you can improve.

- ☑ Offer to help someone tomorrow.

Notes

4. Being Present

Are you here?

> "What is the use of living if it be not to strive for noble causes and to make this world a better place for those who will live in it after we are gone?"
> -Winston Churchill

My Story

Reflecting on my corporate experiences, a great deal of time was spent in meetings. These meetings ranged from one-on-ones to teams of ten or twenty to business reviews that involved hundreds. Each meeting was an opportunity—but I did not always see them that way. Instead, I viewed them as an interruption preventing me from getting to the real work.

I realize now how impactful having a real presence can be and what my focus and attention during those meetings could have meant. After all of my experiences and experiments trying to get my voice heard, get my hands dirty, and be noticed, I missed it. The best way to be seen as a key contributor is to really be present, and *actually* contribute something.

Have you ever been called on at a meeting and not known the question or even the main topic being reviewed? Or have you ever been a presenter and looked across an audience of blank stares? I have experienced both scenarios and they are equally discourteous and inefficient. Just think about how our experiences in these situations might have improved if we concentrated on looking for opportunities to demonstrate our knowledge, show support, and contribute in a meaningful way. It is amazing how much we can accomplish when we choose to focus on the moment and fully engage. It really does pay to put the iPhone or Blackberry away and pay attention to the people around us. When we bring our full, present selves to the table, great things can be accomplished in an efficient and extraordinary way.

Here's a new strategy I have been implementing and sharing with my coaching clients that has had great results: ASK THREE QUESTIONS.

- One that offers support and encouragement
- One that asks for clarification of a particular subject
- One that demonstrates the vital inclusionary behavior of successful leaders

Go into the next meeting with the intention of asking three questions and look for opportunities to do so with those three things in mind. I'm sure you'll see a change taking place in what you learn and how people think about your participation in the meeting.

What "Presence" Really Means

As leaders, we have a responsibility to fully participate; it **not only benefits us as individuals, but facilitates the engagement of others.** We set the standard. At your next meeting, look into the eyes of those at the table. Are the high beams on? If not, what will it take for you to help them snap out of their stupor and fully engage? Ask questions that will demonstrate that you care about their contribution. After all, why did you invite them to the meeting? To take up space? No! You invited them because you wanted their opinion—you knew they had experience, knowledge, and a creative approach that would be valuable to the whole.

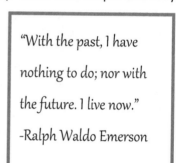

"With the past, I have nothing to do; nor with the future. I live now."

-Ralph Waldo Emerson

Without these participants, the team cannot be complete. Through your own distracted or multitasking behavior, you are allowing and even encouraging others to act as though they are off the hook.

You have the capability to change "business as usual" into business as "meaningful." Recreate your workplace into a community where everyone contributes their talents with passion and purpose. And make sure you foster an open environment where people are allowed to share their thoughts and ideas without fear of judgment. There are NO stupid questions and NO stupid ideas.

Set expectations based on your behavior and others will follow your lead. Be an active and engaged leader; show 'em what you've got!

Presence By Example

One of the most powerful things about being present is what it does for those around you. By being fully present we honor, support, and respect the employees and coworkers that we come into contact with. As leaders, we create a workplace that cares deeply for everyone's success. And consequently, everyone works as a team to create a mutual success.

Help your team rise above the fear of failure by showing them you are willing to unabashedly share your thoughts, strategies, and insights. Be strong! By creating a powerful example of open and engaged leadership, you will enable others to also open themselves up to their full potential. **These individuals are waiting for you, the LEADER, to establish some room for growth**—to set the stage.

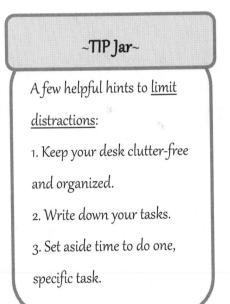

~TIP Jar~

A few helpful hints to limit

distractions:

1. Keep your desk clutter-free

and organized.

2. Write down your tasks.

3. Set aside time to do one,

specific task.

The 90 Minute Focus Challenge

"Human beings are not computers. They are meant to pulse." Those are the words of Tony Schwartz, President and CEO of the Energy Project, an initiative that focuses on fostering creativity and productivity in the lives of modern workers. According to Schwartz, human beings are built to work in cycles, not in one continuous streak like computers. We have peak times—when our minds and bodies are energized and performing at their best—and we also have off-peak times, when we are exhausted and in need of rest and rejuvenation. Modern business culture tends to overlook the importance of renewing our personal energy and, as a result, we have trouble staying present.

> "The culture of distraction is rewiring our brains, making us less happy, less able to connect with people and form a conscience."
>
> -A.J. Jacobs, Blogger for "Real Simple"

Many people believe that the way to get through their busy work day is to tackle several different projects at the same time. We have become a culture of multi-taskers: checking our email on the road, updating our Twitter accounts during business meetings, video-chatting with our colleagues while doing other work. And when we grow weary, we gulp down a cup of coffee or a five-hour energy shot and keep on going. Frankly, it's not working. We are often tired, unhappy, and producing subpar results. Instead, Schwartz recommends this alternative:

"**Work in ninety-minute increments. Do *one* thing at a time in an absorbed way for a significant period of time. Then take a break.**"

Schwartz emphasizes "break time." It is important for our bodies to relax and repair themselves and our minds to find a few moments of peace. And why ninety minutes? Several studies have shown that ninety minutes is the optimal amount of time for human beings to hold their concentration and focus on a single task.

There is no magic way to let your body repair and renew. Our bodies are unique and we all need to relax in different ways and for different lengths of time. That said, here are some of my personal suggestions for creating a little peace for yourself during the day:

- Read a few pages of a book or magazine
- Eat a sit-down lunch *away* from your desk
- Take a short walk outside or, if it is January in Minnesota, do a few loops around your office
- Call your mother! (or a friend or your children)
- Take several deep breaths; focus on clearing your lungs and your mind
- Engage your brain: Do the daily crossword or Sudoku

If you practice inserting a few little breaks between designated work times, you should begin to notice a difference in your ability to stay present. Focus on one task at a time, do it well, and reward yourself every ninety minutes. By breaking your day into bite-sized pieces, it will be easier to perform meaningful work and stay focused.

Conference Calls Come to Life

Conference calls—what a dilemma! These calls are necessary for connecting the global community, cost-effectively reaching a broad audience, and communicating quickly. But what percentage of your audience is completely focused on the content of the call? I am guessing very few. So, how can you improve this sparse participation? How can you engage your co-workers and encourage creativity and idea-generation?

There are tactics you can employ as a leader to improve this stagnant participation. One great way to get people listening, talking, and maybe even laughing is to **make your conference calls more interactive**. Involve more people in the call. Ask questions that prompt electronic responses. This allows you to gauge your audience participation. You may not know the "who," but you will get a feel for the percentage of people engaged. Another way to encourage interaction is simply to change participants' geography. One example: Ask attendees to close their computers and move to a different room in the office. You may even ask those participants near you to join you in your office.

When I was newly hired at one organization, I was invited to be part of a regularly-scheduled conference call on Monday mornings with the sales team. We all remained in our offices for the call, even though six of us were in offices on the same floor. I was glad to be invited to participate in the call and viewed it as an opportunity to gain credibility and get to know the team. After two calls I had not successfully made my voice heard, nor gotten to know anyone. Looking for a solution to this challenge, I asked if we could reserve a conference room for the call AND asked to have five minutes on the agenda. Being together gave me the opportunity to interact with the home office team. Having time on the agenda, though brief, let me share an update on my projects and allowed me to build relationships with the people in field organization that would be contributors to my work.

After two conference calls held together, I began getting calls from the field sales management with ideas and observations. The connections that were made by establishing my presence encouraged and enabled others to support me. The input I got following calls helped me launch a much better program and the accountability of the sales team was enhanced because they knew the person connected to their results. The relationships I developed were invaluable. I also felt much more connected to the home office team and learned the business faster. Another benefit of holding conference calls this way was the ability of the local team to mute the phone, make a decision together, and solve problems without having to hold another meeting. Whew! See how "slow" can be fast?

In the midst of all the chaos, let's breathe and acknowledge each other. Be present; get things done.

Your arsenal

- ☑ Take the 90-minute challenge. Break your day into bite-sized pieces and set aside time for maximum focus and minimal distractions. Take note of how much you accomplish.

- ☑ Go to tomorrow's meeting with the intention of asking questions—be the leader by closing your computer and opening your notebook instead.

- ☑ Identify two of your greatest distractions and brainstorm ways to minimize their impact on your time and effectiveness.

- ☑ Identify two people in your organization who have demonstrated potential, seem interesting, and who you wish you knew better. Resolve to build these relationships by showing interest or appreciation.

- ☑ Revamp conference calls! Brainstorm ideas with your colleagues about how to better engage participants.

Notes

5. Balancing Your Heart and Your Head

Lead with Compassion

> "In a world obsessed with 'what do I get,'
> we must begin to ask a new question,
> which is 'what do I have to give?'"
>
> -John Hope Bryant,
> Author of *Love Leadership*

My Story

Story One: Fear-Based Leadership

Recently, a coaching client opened up to me about his anxiety and concern associated with interactions among his work team and supervisor. He told me that meetings in his office are particularly intimidating because of the cynical comments his co-workers tend to make when someone shares an idea or thought. They might say, "And who made you so smart?" or "What makes you think that we are interested in *that*?" He explained that he is almost afraid to help problem-solve or bring forward a finding from his research because he will be made to feel stupid or foolish.

To make matters worse, the snide comments and pessimistic attitudes extend beyond the meeting room. If, for example, he stops by his supervisors cube to ask a question or make an offer, he is often met with a bored stare and told, "This had better be worth my time."

While my coaching client shared these stories with me, I was dumbfounded. Where do I start to help him navigate the situation? How could I possibly help him surmount such a mountain of negativity? I was really close to suggesting that he quit, but I knew that was *not* the right answer. Besides, I think he had already considered that option and had decided to face his hostile workplace, rather than succumb to it.

Fear comes at us in a variety of ways: Fear of the unknown, fear of failure, fear of being embarrassed. All fear slows us down, holds us back, and prevents us from being and doing our best. In this case, my client and I talked about what he was afraid of and how he could manage that fear. I also asked him, "What's the worst that could happen when you're faced with disinterest or opposition?" I asked a million (at least it felt that way) questions and he gradually began to create a plan for persevering in his work environment and listening to the positive comments (and not focusing on the negative talk) coming from his co-workers.

Making people feel inferior, especially if it is intentional or meant to "put them in their place" does nothing to help us as leaders. It only creates an atmosphere of fear and anxiety, pushes people away, and causes them to either give up or desperately seek external help. Fortunately for his company, my client chose to pursue counseling and create a proactive career plan; he could have easily just thrown in the towel.

Story Two: Love-Based Leadership

To begin, I have a few questions for you. My intention is not to make you feel guilty or inadequate, but to help you reflect on your leadership style and motivate you to show genuine care for your employees. Let me ask you...

Do you take your heart to work? Do your employees see your human, caring side? Are you actively engaged in attempting to understand others? When you hear about a hardship that someone has faced, do you drop a note or a card on their desk? Do you make a point of showing others you genuinely care?

I have often been astounded by the difference a little compassion can make. There were times when I reached out to troubled employees—through cards, flowers, or attending a loved one's funeral—and received deep gratitude and friendship in return. Other times, I did not receive a thing. Regardless, I know I am doing the right thing by making a kind gesture or lending a helping hand. And, when I had some tough times (illness and unexpected deaths), peers, leaders, and my employees were there for me as well. It made the situation better knowing I was surrounded with people that cared about me and my well being.

There are times when we need a nudge to do the right thing. As a regional sales leader I held quarterly meetings with my management team. These meetings typically were for the purpose of strategy alignment, team building, personal growth, etc. One time, I was gathered for a three-day conference with a team of eight managers which I led in the eastern United States.

The final day of our meetings also happened to be when my youngest son was "graduating" from sixth grade and headed to junior high the following September. As we were beginning our meeting and doing a little check-in, I mentioned my son's event. My team remarked, "Why are you here?" I shrugged and said, "It's *only* sixth grade." In return, they asked, "Will he graduate from sixth grade again?" "Gosh, I hope not!" I laughed and the meeting went on as planned. But the next morning when I walked into the conference room, my team handed me a new flight itinerary, told me they changed my flight during the night, and I was leaving the next morning at five o'clock. They would handle the meeting wrap up; they wanted me to go home and get to the graduation. I was stunned, grateful, and proud. I had employees that trusted me and knew me well enough to know that making such a bold move wasn't a career ending move, but something that actually bonded our team and made me forever thankful to them. My son was happy to see me, too!

Why Lead With Love?

As a leader, you have a choice. You can choose to hold your employees and team-members under your thumb, insisting they silently follow your pre-determined expectations OR you can choose to listen to your staff, show a genuine interest in their ideas (and their lives), and collaborate with them on projects and goals. I call these two leadership styles "fear-based" and "love-based." We live in a competitive, high-speed, and cut-throat time. Many companies are genuinely concerned about their bottom-line and if they are going to turn a profit next quarter. In such an environment, it is easy to encounter fear-based leaders or become one yourself.

But does it really matter? Does your leadership style really make a difference in today's business world? The short answer: yes. Yes, it matters. And the difference between the two styles can be profound.

Ray Williams, leadership development advisor and author of *The Leadership Edge* and *Breaking Bad Habits*, emphasizes the pitfalls of fear-based leadership and the importance of being a kind and compassionate leader. He says, "Recent research on successful leaders and the current turbulent economic and social times calls out for a different style of leader—one that exhibits kindness, compassion, and empathy. **Driving, directive, coercive styles of leadership may move people and get results in the short-term, but the dissonance it creates is associated with toxic relationships and emotions such as anger, anxiety, and fear.**"

> "Happiness is not just something nice to have; it can also become the centerpiece of your business strategy."
>
> -Chade-Meng Tan

If you want results tomorrow, fear-based leadership may work. However, if you want to build a sustainable company model and retain a dedicated and highly-motivated staff, love-based leadership is a better choice. Repeatedly, studies have shown that effective and compassionate leadership is linked to positive company growth. One prime example is Google's business model. Google actively encourages free-thinking, open lines of communication, and the use of creativity to solve problems. They even have a social responsibility team, as well as an internally-created and operated program dedicated to compassionate leadership and empathy called "Search Inside Yourself."

Such initiatives are not a fad. Leading through love and empathy has proven to be an effective model for sustainable company growth. This leadership approach has been linked to higher productivity among workers, reduced sick days, and better overall physical and mental health. No one wants to be the kind of boss who raises her employees' blood pressure.

The Open Door

You can most likely identify a troubled workplace when you see one: the closed office doors, the harried looks, the guilty glances when employees slip out the door for lunch or to make a quick telephone call to handle personal business. This type of secretive, closed environment is anything but sustainable. You can't retain employees that are constantly stressed and stifled. People need room to breathe. They need room for creativity and growth. They need room to make mistakes and learn from them. Frankly, people need an environment where they can be...well, people.

As a compassionate leader, it is your job to both direct your staff and give them the freedom to make their own contributions to the company. One of the ways to accomplish this is by thinking in terms of "we" versus "I." Even if you would like to be the only king in the castle, remember workplaces rely on connectivity and interaction with others. You are a part of a team and your choices do not just impact yourself. Think about how you can collaborate with others on various projects or resolutions. Instead of making decisions behind closed doors, have a meeting. Gather the players who will be affected by a certain decision or initiative and open the floor to discussion. The more voices that are heard, the greater the chance of finding an innovative and effective solution to a problem.

One of the keys to creating a collaborative working environment is by making people comfortable to share their thoughts and opinions. It is important to promote a workplace that is **transparent, honest, and open**. It starts with you. Think about how you perform your daily tasks. Do you work in an office by yourself and have little interaction with co-workers? Even if you are uncomfortable working with your door *physically* open, it doesn't mean you shouldn't keep your door *metaphorically* open. Create open lines of communication with those that work underneath you. Keep track of their tasks and ask them questions about their progress. And don't just send an email; stop by their office for a couple minutes. It's amazing what

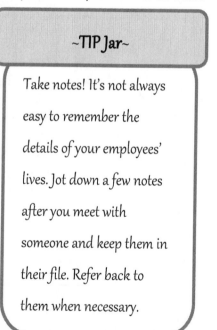

~TIP Jar~

Take notes! It's not always easy to remember the details of your employees' lives. Jot down a few notes after you meet with someone and keep them in their file. Refer back to them when necessary.

a difference a little face-time can make.

You have the power to retain happy, healthy employees. *You* have the power to foster a positive, open, and collaborative environment. But don't forget to set boundaries. Don't forget you're still the boss.

Leading With Your Heart (and Your Head)

In the business world, we are sometimes warned against "thinking with our hearts." No one wants to be identified as a softy or a pushover. No boss wants their employees to walk all over them and get away with poor productivity or lax office conduct. I wholeheartedly agree. There is a difference between love-based leadership and soft leadership. **Effective love-based leadership is rooted in compassion and empathy, but also sets boundaries**. You can be a caring leader *and* hold your employees to high expectations at the same time. The two are not mutually exclusive. It can, however, be a balancing act.

As a love-based leader, you have to be certain that both your expectations and boundaries are clear. If they are not, the line between "boss" and "friend" might be muddled or your employees might begin to let their productivity slip. By drawing a firm line in the sand, you can send the message that yes, you are a compassionate leader, but you are not there to mess around. There is work that needs to be done and you need people who can do it. But how do you draw such a line?

Setting up boundaries is often easier said than done. Once you become close with your employees, it may be difficult to correct their work or actions. If you reach this point with any of your employees, you're going to have to dial down the "friendship knob" a bit and amp up the "boss knob." You can continue to listen to them, learn about them, and care about them, but you do not have to be their buddy.

One effective way to balance your heart-leadership with your head is to conduct regular meetings with your employees. Maybe it's not possible to meet with everyone on a regular basis, but make sure you have one-on-one conferences with your key players and keep those conferences open and candid. Ask open-ended questions that allow your employees the freedom to reply with more than a yes or no answer. Try to meet at least once a month or once a quarter (depending on the size of your company and the number of people that work directly beneath you). Know what they're up to!

By keeping track of your employees' tasks and accomplishments, you will not only show a genuine interest in their work, you will also hold them accountable. If one of your employees does not meet her goals this month, get to the root of the problem. Ask her why she thinks she didn't meet your expectations and then brainstorm ideas together to come up with a game plan for next month. Be sure to let her know that you are counting on her to meet the revised goal and if she encounters a problem along the way, she needs to bring it to your attention immediately. Ask how you can help.

Your employees should not have to wonder about their personal performance. As a savvy leader, you need to create a logical, straight-forward system to measure employee performance. If you're in sales or marketing, that measurement will most likely be in dollars. If you're in a different field, such as customer service, perhaps your measurements will be based off of customer surveys. Or a personalized scorecard that you create for your employees, where you measure their performance in different key areas based on a scale of 1 to 10. Meet with your staff regularly and share their "report cards" with them. That way, your expectations are clear and you can have an open and candid conversation about your employee's progress.

> "Good leaders make people feel that they're at the very heart of things, not at the periphery. Everyone feels that he or she makes a difference to the success of the organization. When that happens, people feel centered and that gives their work meaning."
>
> -Warren Bennis

Just because you choose to lead from your heart, doesn't mean you can't use your head. Practice smart leadership, practice savvy leadership, and care about your co-workers every step of the way.

Your arsenal

☑ Think about a time when you experienced the impact of fear-based leadership. How might this instance have turned out differently with love-based leadership? Jot down some ideas.

☑ What's on your calendar tomorrow? Think about how you can include co-workers in your plans. Then, do it!

☑ Identify employees who do not usually speak up during meetings or other group work. Make a point to hear their voices during your next meeting.

☑ Learn at least three personal facts about each co-worker. Keep a notebook or spreadsheet of these facts and refer back to them before you meet with any given employee.

☑ Follow-up in person. Instead of shooting Jim an email, walk down the hall and have a conversation with him face-to-face.

Notes

---

6. No Excuses

No One is Buying It.

> "He that is good for making excuses is
> seldom good at anything else."
> -Benjamin Franklin

My Story

"No excuses" doesn't just mean having the courage to take responsibility for mistakes you've made or deadlines you've missed. It also means setting yourself up for success and putting yourself in a position where you won't have to make excuses. I have been guilty of taking on too much work or throwing myself into the thick of a project that I did not feel fully prepared to do. I've also found myself making excuses for my work because my client's expectations simply did not align with my own.

At one point, I was asked to revise a résumé for a client. I had experience reworking résumés for many people hailing from a variety of different professions, so I had no doubt that I was fully qualified for the task. However, trouble started brewing when our expectations collided. She and I had entirely different visions for how the project was supposed to go. I expected feedback and input from her about our progress; she expected me to revise her résumé and spit it out, complete with jargon that was specific to her profession. Right out of the gate, we began to butt heads.

To complicate matters, my client was not amenable to many of the changes I made to her résumé and was perplexed at my insistence to whittle it down from six pages to one or two. She resisted when I suggested cutting some of the content and was quick to criticize any grammatical or punctuation errors the first draft contained. I found myself defending my work tooth and nail and making up excuses for any piece she considered to be subpar. Then, I took a step back and examined the situation.

The problem was not my work. The problem was not her perspective. Instead, it stemmed from a basic misunderstanding of each other's approach to the project and the end-goals we wanted to achieve. Instead of making excuses for my work, I should have been asking questions to get to the heart of our disagreement such as, "How do you envision the end product?" Or, "How would you have revised this section differently?" Instead, we ended up clashing and I learned a valuable lesson on aligning expectations and setting the stage for successful client interactions, free from explanations and excuses.

Saying Yes to the Right Things

Why do we make excuses? Is it because we *actually* believe people will fall for our tall-tales and exaggerations? Is it because we think excuses will *improve* our reputation? Absolutely not. We make excuses because we are embarrassed by our mistakes or shortcomings and fall back on our natural human instinct to cover our tracks. But why make those mistakes in the first place? Why put ourselves in awkward positions from which we have to claw our way out? The answer: we really don't have to. By a little savvy self-management, we can usually (life happens, after all!) eliminate those palm-sweating situations that require tiresome explanations. It starts with a little clear thinking.

Before you make a new commitment—whether it be leading a team project, starting a new job with a long commute, or taking on a new client—take some time to evaluate the situation. **Ask yourself these three basic questions:**

1. Do I have the time?
2. Do I have the motivation?
3. Do I have the qualifications or necessary support?

If you answered yes to all three questions, great. Nothing should stop you from excelling at your new project and achieving your goals. If you answered no to one or more of the above questions, slow down! Think. Evaluate. Ask yourself what might get in the way of your success. Do you have the motivation, but are short on time? Think about how you might juggle your schedule to create more time. Is it worth it? Will other projects or commitments suffer? Is your sacrifice only short-term?

This is your time to do a little soul searching and ask if you're setting yourself up for victory or excuse-riddled failure. Just like laying a solid foundation is key to building a sturdy home, so too is setting up good parameters necessary for new projects. If the foundation isn't there—time, motivation, qualifications—chances are you'll find yourself making excuses for your performance.

In short, think before saying yes.

Saying No

It isn't easy to say no. You don't want to let your boss or co-workers down. You don't want to appear weak or unmotivated. Frankly, you don't want to be fired. But sometimes you have to have a little courage to stand up and Just Say No.

It's all well and good to be a yes-man in the short term. People will appreciate your willingness to tackle any project, no matter what it is. However, this approach to your career is **unhealthy, unsustainable, and, in the end, unrewarding**. Saying yes to every project and then failing to deliver on a third of them is much worse than saying no to a project that you are simply not prepared to handle.

> "I do not know the key to success, but the key to failure is trying to please everybody." -Bill Cosby

I'm not saying that you shouldn't stretch yourself. Clearly, you are capable of great things with the proper amount of focus and planning. But there is a difference between reaching beyond your comfort zone and agreeing to take on a fifth project when you're already struggling to stay on top of projects one through four.

So, pause. Think about what lies before you. Is your boss' request realistic? Is it something you are capable of doing? Are you already bogged down with other projects? It is possible that some of the snags can be worked out and, with a few modifications, you can tackle the project after all? Maybe a deadline needs to be extended. Or maybe some extra help needs to enlisted. Before deciding to say no, consider your options and the flexibility of the project.

Let's say the deadline cannot be extended or the project cannot be modified and you feel filled to the gills with assignments, client meetings, and presentation preps. Now is the time to say no. When you turn down a project or decline a potential new client, **say no gracefully**. Do not send an email to your boss or whoever assigned you the project. Instead, schedule a face-to-face meeting. It is surprising how many miscommunications occur over email or texting. Not only is it difficult to judge a person's tone or inflection in writing, it is also tedious to ask clarifying questions or offer comments. It is better (and often more efficient) to set aside some time to meet in the same room. And if that's not possible, pick up the phone.

~TIP Jar~

Tactful "No" Phrases:

"The main reason I am forced to decline..."

"At this time, I believe it is in my best interest..."

"I gave the situation a lot of thought and have concluded..."

When you meet with your boss/potential new client/co-workers, do not forget to come prepared. Create an outline of what you're going to say, detailing your reasons for declining the new assignment. Be clear and concise. Explain that you have given the situation a lot of thought and have concluded that there is little chance of you doing your best work given the circumstances. Also, anticipate questions. Think about what kinds of things the other party is likely to ask and brainstorm clear, logical, and honest answers.

And stand your ground! If your boss starts to make you feel guilty for not picking up the assignment, do not get defensive or intimidated. Do not cave in to her pushing. Instead, calmly repeat your reasons for declining and emphasize the fact that you care about the company's success. If you were to push ahead with the project (knowing full well that you are ill-equipped to do so), how would your company possibly benefit?

Offer alternative solutions for the task at hand. Come up with a handful of ideas that could possibly keep the project afloat. It may be as simple as, "What if we wait another three months before I attempt this project?" OR "Have you considered asking Christina if she'd like to do that additional research? She has expressed interest in that kind of work in the past."

Show that you care. Show that you are not just going to abandon your team and let them flounder around with a misplaced project. By offering alternative solutions, you are demonstrating that you care enough about your company's well-being to take the time to think about potential ways to keep the project alive. Make it clear that you are still an integral part of the company and you want to see it succeed.

As a final tip, make *sure* you do your very best with the projects you have. It is difficult to say no to a project and there is a possibility you will take some flak for doing so, BUT all that will most likely be forgotten if you continue to work hard on your current assignments and prove you can get the job done. Remember, you create your own success.

Your "No Excuses" Action Plan

Even if you have carefully assessed a new project and have started things off on the right foot, set-backs can happen. That's life. Maybe your personal life causes you to have trouble focusing on your projects. Maybe you have a change in management at work and you find it difficult to collaborate with your new boss. Or maybe you delve into a project and realize you are not fully qualified to do a stellar job. These things happen. In fact, you should *expect* them to happen. The important question to ask yourself is this:

"How do I deal with the bumps in the road?"

One thing is certain, <u>excuses</u> is not the right answer!

If you find yourself derailed and need to get back on track, take some time to yourself. Find a quiet space and begin to work on an **Action Plan** that will renew your chances of success. When you create your action plan, consider the following items:

1. Determine what is throwing you off course

Take the time to identify what is holding you back from performing at your peak. Is it something you can control? Or is it out of your hands? Is your obstacle mostly mental or attitude-related? How easy will it be to overcome your challenges?

2. Have an honest conversation

Have an open and honest conversation with yourself (it often helps to write things down or make a list of your concerns!) and with those involved in your project. First, jot down a few things that are troubling you about the current project, and then list a few possible solutions to your troubles. Once you have collected your thoughts, talk to the other people that are involved in the project. Just initiating an open dialogue can work wonders when things are feeling a little off-track. Remember to *not only* present your own ideas, but *listen* to the ideas of others. Who knows what solutions your colleagues might offer? Let yourself be open to their thoughts before you decide on a course of action.

3. Ask good questions

One of the keys to getting your project back on track and making sure everyone involved is on the same page is to ask thoughtful questions. If you are finding a new boss or client difficult to work with, ask open-ended questions like, "How would you like this project to turn out?" or "What kind of progress would you like to see by next week? Next month?" or "What role do you see me taking as this project moves forward?" By asking dialogue-creating questions, you will be able to gain a better understanding of the direction of your project and what you need to do to make the key players happy.

4. Set goals/milestones

Once you have considered your hurdles and have brain-stormed ideas on how to get your assignment heading in the right direction again, set goals. <u>Are you having trouble meeting your deadlines</u>? Lay out a plan in bite-sized pieces and stick to it. Use a calendar and be sure to include some wiggle-room to make up for days that were less productive than you planned. <u>Are you finding it difficult to meet your new client's expectations</u>? Once you have had an honest conversation with your client (see step 2), write down all of his expectations on a chart and post it on the wall. Refer back to the chart daily and make sure you are working to meet the set goals. <u>Are you finding part of your work tedious or difficult?</u> Once you have had an open dialogue (again, step 2) and have determined you still **want to** and **can** tackle the project, lay out the steps you will take for finding qualified assistance. Maybe you need to lean on your co-workers' expertise. Maybe you need to take a class to refresh your knowledge. Make sure your plan is **manageable, realistic, and broken down** into steps. Don't forget to reward yourself for each accomplishment!

You've created your action plan and have gotten back on target, keep in mind that it is not fail-safe. Deadlines might still slip through the cracks; expectations might not be fully met. How you deal with these bumps in the road is what truly matters. Instead of making excuses and dancing around your dilemmas, confront them head-on. Make a new action plan. Have an open dialogue with those involved. Your co-workers and clients will most likely respect you for your honesty and appreciate your transparency. And you can feel better about yourself knowing that are doing everything you can to eliminate the need for excuses.

Your arsenal

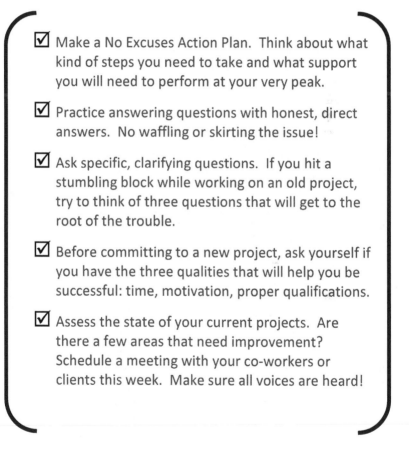

- ☑ Make a No Excuses Action Plan. Think about what kind of steps you need to take and what support you will need to perform at your very peak.

- ☑ Practice answering questions with honest, direct answers. No waffling or skirting the issue!

- ☑ Ask specific, clarifying questions. If you hit a stumbling block while working on an old project, try to think of three questions that will get to the root of the trouble.

- ☑ Before committing to a new project, ask yourself if you have the three qualities that will help you be successful: time, motivation, proper qualifications.

- ☑ Assess the state of your current projects. Are there a few areas that need improvement? Schedule a meeting with your co-workers or clients this week. Make sure all voices are heard!

Notes

7. Having Clarity
A Clear Vision, Clearly Stated.

> "It's a lack of clarity that creates
> chaos and frustration. Those emotions
> are poison to any living goal."
> -Steve Maraboli,
> *Life, the Truth, and Being Free*

My Story

The backbone of any business organization is its vision statement or mission statement. When a company is working towards a common goal—whether that be providing superb and consistent customer service or manufacturing quality and affordable products—there is unity and purpose behind its employees' actions. If a business vision is clear, articulate, and kept at the forefront of people's minds, it gives them a sense that they are working towards something, a common goal.

A great example of a living mission statement can be found at a local banking giant. Their basic vision is, "We want to satisfy all our customers' financial needs and help them succeed financially." A simple statement, yes, but they decided to take their fourteen word statement and expand it into a "Vision and Values Handbook." This handbook makes their basic vision come alive by detailing the actions they will take in order to work towards their goals. To further emphasize the importance of their vision and values, retail employees meet on a regular basis and refer to the handbook, aligning the work they do with their purpose. It is a constant reminder that each employee is key to meeting their overarching goal. In short, a clear company vision and mission statement are important and should be kept alive throughout the organization.

When a local women's business organization approached me with the request to revise their outdated vision statement, I gladly accepted. This organization had experienced several significant changes in its focus and scope. The leadership team came to the realization that their organization's written vision was no longer as accurate and inclusive as they wanted it to be.

So, we went about crafting a message that would correctly and succinctly reflect the organization's values, goals, and membership scope. I worked with about ten women from the leadership team on this project for almost thirty hours. Language is a touchy thing and we wanted to make sure we were accurately articulating our purpose and direction. We also wanted to make a statement that had staying power. Would our words be just as relevant ten years down the road? Twenty? Fifty? Of course, it's impossible to say, but some statements hold up better than others. We tested our ideas during small group meetings and surveys within the greater organization.

When we finished working out our statement, it was time for the small group to present the idea to the rest of the organization—about eighty-five members in total. Generally, people do not like change, so presenting a new idea can be a challenge. However, we laid out our entire thought process, walked the other members through our ideas, and carefully explained our word choices. We built a solid case for change and, in the end, our refreshed vision statement was met with overwhelming support. I attribute our success to clarity. We focused on creating a clear vision statement *and* clearly explaining our choices to the larger group. By taking the time to focus on clarity, we avoided all the confusion, resistance, and wasted time that comes with ambiguity.

Clear Goals; Clear Vision

Leaders deal with a lot of unknowns. For instance, they might not know how certain changes will affect their company's growth or their employees' morale. Or they might not know how the marketplace will change over the course of the next year and affect their business. Leaders are obligated to concern themselves with the future of their company and the future, of course, is an uncertain place.

Good leaders take on the burden of uncertainty themselves and attempt to **articulate an end goal or a clear vision** for the employees working for them. Even though you might be handed a vague assignment or a poorly-defined goal by your superiors and asked to create a plan to reach the assigned goal, you do not have to pass the

> "Singleness of purpose is one of the chief essentials for success in life, no matter what may be one's aim."
>
> -John D. Rockefeller, Jr.

ambiguity off to your employees. For example, if your supervisor tells you the company needs to see significant growth next year or they'll have to start making cuts, you can take that vague objective, create a set of parameters for it, and present it to your team in a way that motivates them instead of confuses or discourages them. Instead of saying, "Look guys, we all have to work harder this year to increase our company growth," say, "Our goal is to increase sales revenue by six percent this year across the board. There are several ways we can get there, but we are looking to all of you first to brainstorm some ideas for how this growth can be achieved."

A clearly defined goal will give your employees something to aim for—a tangible target to focus on and work towards. The opportunity to be part of the plan to get there creates commitment and support. Otherwise, your people are likely to flounder. They will not have the same sense of

> *"Clarity affords focus."*
>
> -Thomas Leonard

purpose behind their work or the same sense of direction if they do not feel as if they are working towards and contributing to a distinct end goal.

But choose your end goal wisely. If you are given an assignment such as, "increase company growth" or "decrease project turnaround time" or "build a larger client base," you must take the time to mull these objectives over. What might your supervisor mean by "build a larger client base?" Do they want you to go about courting several new clients? Or amplifying sales from existing clients? Or perhaps a combination of both? Ask clarifying questions in order to understand what your superiors are *really* looking for. Attempt to understand the thought process that led them to create this particular objective. After you have a clear understanding of the goal, think about how you can define it in a way that will motivate others. **The more specific the goal, the better.** For instance, "We need to add at least four more clients as well as sell an additional forty thousand dollars worth of services by the end of the fiscal year." Do your research: figure out how many clients your company will have to add and how much additional revenue it will need in order to sustain growth. Then aim high, but not so high that your team feels overwhelmed or discouraged.

Once you have defined and articulated your goal, it is time to take a step back. Place a little trust in your employees (see chapter three) and let them figure out the best path or paths to attain the given objective. Although the end point should be clear, the route to get there does not have to be so well-defined. In fact, it is better if it is not. Part of having clarity is **keeping a clear mind** and **knowing when you can step away** from a project in order to allow others to take ownership of it.

If you have done your job correctly from the get-go (if you have clearly and concisely delivered a set of specific objectives to your employees), then you should have little to worry about when you remove yourself from the center of the assignment. Trust your employees. Let them brainstorm solutions for achieving the end goals you have laid out for them. Perhaps their ideas will take them down a different path from the one you initially had in mind, but that's ok! If their plan seems feasible, then go for it. When people feel like they are playing a significant role in a project—when they feel like they own it, so to speak— they are more likely to be motivated and energized to work. They own the project; they are an integral part of it; they are an important asset to the company. Can you imagine how productive people would be if they went to work every morning feeling this way?

What I Say VS. What You Hear

Unfortunately, having a clear vision and developing a clear set of goals is only part of the battle. Another crucial aspect of having clarity in the workplace has to do with delivering and receiving messages. Ambiguity, misinterpretation, or lack of understanding can all cause costly delays or undue worry. It is much more efficient to **take the time to deliver a clear and detailed message** than to rush past the details and expect others to understand your motives and intentions.

Take, for instance, this simple email message sent by Joan, division supervisor:

Martha,
I would like to meet with you in my office tomorrow at 4:00.
-Joan

How will Martha interpret Joan's email? On one hand, she might think, "Terrific, I have been meaning to speak with Joan about some of the recent changes in my workload. This is my opportunity to talk to her and ask her a few questions." Or, she might think, "Oh great, the company is making cuts again and this time I'm the one about to get the axe. I have a daughter who needs new hockey equipment and a son who needs braces. This is terrible news!"

Martha's reaction to Joan's vague and uninformative email will undoubtedly depend on her mood and current circumstances. It might affect her productivity for the rest of the day or cause her to be distracted. Whatever the case, valuable human resources could be wasted by unfounded worry or stress.

Imagine if everyone in the office received a similar email message from Joan, each with a different meeting time. Now, you've got a pandemic on your hands. People naturally speculate and talk about the unknown and imagine an end state far worse than reality. Better that Joan take the time to lay out exactly what she is after:

Martha,
I would like to meet with you in my office tomorrow at 4:00 for a twenty minute meeting regarding our new client, ABC, Inc. I'd like to share what I've learned about their business model and give you the chance to ask any questions you might have regarding the company or your specific role in relation to this new client. I will be meeting with everyone in the division over the next few days, so please arrive promptly at your allotted time.
Thanks,
-Joan

In this version of the email to Martha, Joan has been careful to lay out relevant details regarding tomorrow's meeting. She has anticipated the questions Martha might ask (What is the meeting about? How should I prepare? When is the meeting? How long will it last? Who else will be meeting with Joan?) and has preemptively answered them all in her email. Now, Martha can take a few minutes to prepare for the meeting, mark it on her calendar, and then carry on with the rest of her day. No time wasted; no unnecessary stress.

Don't Shoot the Messenger

The same clarity should be used when you are delivering a new plan or project to your employees. Many people do not like change and it may take some convincing for them to get on board with a new idea or new way of doing things. They might wonder, "What was wrong with the old system?" or, "Will the new system really work?" The best thing to do is walk people through the thought process that led to the initiation of a new project. Remember, you've probably been thinking about and working on this plan for quite some time and your co-workers may be hearing about it for the first time. They need time to process, ask questions, and convince themselves of the validity of the initiative. Once they understand the motive for change and the reasons behind a certain decision, they are more likely to be on board with the change. If you leave them in the dark, you are only creating a breeding ground for gossip, uncertainty, and hesitation.

One method I have used and seen used effectively for delivering new ideas is a three-tiered delivery system. First, the concept is presented to everyone affected by the change. Go over the main points in a large-group setting, allowing for a few questions at the end of the session. Then, break the large group down into smaller groups. Instruct the smaller groups to come up with a list of questions they have about the new project (or policy change or new system, etc.). Then, come back together in a large group and give each small group the opportunity to ask their set of questions. Lastly, meet one-on-one with any employees who still might have questions or concerns about the new project. This gives those uncomfortable in larger group settings a chance to share their thoughts without that intimidation. The goal of this three-tiered system is to **create transparency and openness** around a new project so that everyone involved will feel comfortable tackling it. For some people, the large group presentation is enough, but many people thrive in a small group or one-on-one session and it is up to you, as a leader, to give them an equal opportunity to succeed. Another advantage of this process is that feeling, seeing and hearing other individuals support for the change can convince and motivate additional support without you having to do all of the work.

Asking for Clarity

There are times that you are not on the delivery end of a message but on the receiving end. When you hear, "The company will be employing new technology" or that, "We will be expanding our market to reach a wider customer base," ask questions. If you are unsure about the main point of the project or the reasons behind it, don't be afraid to sit down with one of the decision-makers and attempt to gain some clarity.

Of course, it is in your best interest to be non-confrontational and positive during your interaction. Demonstrate that you support the direction and the well-being of the company, but you need clarification on X, Y, and Z. Attempt to understand the root of the decision by framing your questions like this:

"I can tell you and the other division supervisors have been giving this decision a lot of thought. Would you be willing to review the steps you took to arrive at your decision? I would like to understand it a little better so I can fully support the plan and explain it to others."

-OR-

"I am excited about expanding our business into new markets, but I am still a little confused about X. Would you mind going over that part of the plan in a little more depth with me? I want to be clear on the details so I can prepare for the changes our division will have to make."

Once you are given the additional information, make sure you understand it correctly.

~TIP Jar~

3 Steps to Promote Clarity:

1. Encourage question and answer sessions after meetings

2. Send clear, concise emails

3. Be an example: ask clarifying questions whenever necessary

A good way to ensure clarity is by repeating back what you think you heard. You could say something like, "I want to make sure I understand this correctly. What I think you're saying about the new system is this..." This method of double-checking your understanding of a topic will help ensure that you and the speaker are on the same page. It is another way to be efficient and proactive, and it allows the speaker to clear up any misunder-standings you might have.

Even if you are not crazy about the new projects or new systems that are coming to your office, there is likely more behind the decision than what meets the eye. In the case of a major change, the decision-makers have probably been working on their initiative for months and may not think to go over the details of their thought-processes. It is up to you (the leader!) to be proactive and ask the right questions. Maybe you'll begin to understand the motivation behind a plan. At the very least, you'll be better-informed and better-equipped to handle the upcoming changes.

Above all, demonstrate strong leadership and do NOT join in the fray when others begin complaining about impending changes. You might not agree with every single move your company makes, but grousing about things does not make them better. Instead, stay positive and surround yourself with optimistic people. If, however, you encounter pessimism on your team, do not shy away from it. Have a candid conversation with the cynics and confront them with the same question-asking techniques in order to overcome whatever concerns or issues they might have.

Your arsenal

☑ Are your personal goals and visions clear? You may not be able to control the company's mission statement, but you can certainly write your own.

☑ Get in the habit of re-reading your emails. Have you covered all the necessary details? Is your information clear and to the point?

☑ Next time your supervisor assigns you (or your division) a task, make sure you understand all the details. If something is fuzzy to you, be sure to ask questions! Are you working on the right thing? Don't jump to conclusions.

☑ Practice empathy. Next time you need to present a new idea or give a new assignment, walk your audience through your thought process. Remember that you have spent a lot of time thinking about the given topic, but it is probably their first time hearing about this new information. Anticipate questions that might crop up and attempt to answer them before they are even asked.

Notes

_____

_____

_____

_____

_____

_____

_____

_____

_____

_____

_____

_____

_____

_____

_____

_____

_____

_____

_____

_____

8. Demonstrating Loyalty

What you give is what you get.

> **"A healthy loyalty is not passive and complacent, but active and critical."**
>
> -Harold Laski

My Story

Some of the most rewarding moments in my career were times when I knew, beyond the shadow of a doubt, that I made a difference in someone else's career. We coach, encourage, and push our employees, and then cross our fingers and hope we make a difference. And sometimes there is concrete proof that we *did*, in fact, make a difference.

One such instance occurred when I rode with one of my sales reps on a customer call. We were riding in his car, chatting about his family and the new sales goals for the quarter and the lovely, sunny weather when I noticed something tucked into the car's window visor. I looked closely at the object and saw it was a card addressed to him, written on company paper—a card that I had sent several months earlier.

Every quarter, I recognized my top performing sales reps with a simple thank you note. I always personalized the cards and wrote them out by hand—something I firmly believe makes a huge difference in the level of sincerity of the card. I was careful to pay attention to what projects they were working on or what factors had contributed to their success that quarter and then include a line or two in my card about those observations. In short, I always put a bit of thought into my thank you cards, but didn't necessarily dwell on them for long. I thought they were a nice gesture and figured my employees would read them, appreciate them, and toss them.

"Is that from me?" I asked, pointing at the visor. "I thought everyone just threw those away after a week or two."

He laughed and said, "No, not everyone. That card means a lot to me, Margaret. It's a daily reminder that I can do this job and I'm actually not half bad at it when I put my mind to it. You know, not every day is a knock-'em-out-of-the-park sales day. I need a gentle reminder sometimes that I *can* do this work and I *can* hit my numbers...even if the fish aren't always eager to bite."

I was stunned. I had hoped my thank you cards were making the recipients feel appreciated, but I had no idea they could possess the power to motivate and offer affirmation when the chips were down and they were feeling discouraged with their work. Probably, not everyone was as inspired by my thank you cards as this particular rep, but it meant a lot to me that I had made such a profound difference in his work experience.

The lesson I learned from this and other similar experiences is that small gestures make a big difference. These gestures not only serve to motivate employees and elevate morale, they also build a positive environment that produces loyal employees. An employee who feels appreciated, acknowledged, and who is encouraged to use his or her skills to their maximum potential is more likely to enjoy the work they do *and* do quality work.

It is just as important to *build* this type of employee as it is to *be* this type of employee.

Celebrate the Individual

In the 1960s, it is said that President Kennedy paid a visit to the NASA space center in order to gauge the center's commitment to putting a man on the moon by the end of the decade. As he was walking down the hall, he encountered a janitor sweeping the floor. He paused and introduced himself saying, "Hello, I'm Jack Kennedy. What do you do here at NASA?" The janitor stopped sweeping, looked at Kennedy, and said, "I'm helping to put a man on the moon."

No matter what an individual's role in a company may be, they should always believe they are making an important contribution to the overall mission of the organization. **No job is a small job**. We are all valuable components of our company and if one component fails, we all suffer. Just think about all the people a CEO relies on to do his or her work: computer technicians, custodians, receptionists, accountants, security guards, HVAC specialists, baristas...the list goes on and on. Outstanding leaders take the time to recognize the people that work for them. They make sure those people are acknowledged on an individual level and that they feel as if they are part of something larger than themselves.

An important part of elevating employees' pride in their work is letting them in on the big-picture goals. If your company is working to sell four million dollars worth of products this year, make your people aware of the goal. Hang charts in the hallways that track progress. Send out emails when a milestone is reached. Hold meetings to congratulate individual successes. Your goals should be **apparent, accessible, and measureable**. Even if your business has an abstract mission or big-picture goal such as, "serve all our customers to the best of our ability," you can still acknowledge individual achievements and set up a way to measure your successes. The more keyed-in to the big-picture goals your employees are, the more likely they will feel like the NASA janitor: part of something important and exciting.

Recognize the Individual

Loyal employees feel as if they are 1) making valuable and constructive contributions to the company and 2) recognized for those contributions. As a leader, it is up to you to create an atmosphere that encourages others' strengths and acknowledges their accomplishments. But how?

One of the best (and easiest!) steps you can take is to practice paying attention. Make sure you know what is going on in the office. What projects are your direct reports working on? What are they struggling with? In what areas do they shine? How are they interacting with others? *Do* they interact with others? What motivates them and what holds them back?

If you don't know the answers to all these questions, don't panic! And don't type them up in an email and send them to all your co-workers. Instead, focus on getting to know people. Ask them questions. Be *genuinely interested and caring.* Getting to know your officemates is a long-term project and you can't expect to figure out, for example, what motivates them right off the bat. At the very least, however, you can start tracking the projects your employees are working on and begin to hold one-on-one meetings about their progress. Pay attention to what they say and jot down a few notes (about their attitude towards their projects, anything you learned about their personality, etc.). Keep a file for each employee and refer to it as needed. You might write up something like:

"Karen's sales numbers are slipping and today we discussed possible strategies to get back on track. She will work on improving her rapport with customers and is going to take some time to brainstorm a list of potential new clients. I learned today that Karen's father is in the hospital and she says it is causing additional stress in her life."

So, what should you do next time you see Karen? First and foremost, be a human being. Don't ask her how her sales numbers are looking for the week. Ask her about her father; ask her how she's handling everything. Perhaps, suggest a resource or mentor that can get her back on track. *Then*, refer back to your conversation and ask if she has generated a list of potential new clients. At this point, you can address her lagging sales numbers and give her encouragement to keep at it! Your conversation will have a much greater impact if you show that you **genuinely care** about Karen **on an individual and human level**. She is not just a cog in the machine. She is a living, feeling person and a valuable member of your team. Show her you appreciate her contributions to the company (and you care enough to remember what she said in your last meeting!) and Karen will most likely demonstrate loyalty in return.

As a final note, don't underestimate the power of small gestures. If one of your marketing reps has to travel during his birthday, have a card or some cookies waiting for him in his hotel room. If your accountant's mother passes away, send flowers, or, better yet, go to the memorial service. If it's the end of the quarter and several employees have done outstanding work, send them personalized cards or recognize them in your next group meeting. These acts of kindness might seem small to you, but they are all part of the fabric that comprises a positive, open, and loyal office community.

Light a Fire

Let's talk about motivating people. Motivated employees are loyal employees. They feel as if they are fighting for something— they come to work every day with a little bit of fire under their shoes and continue working hard to achieve some goal or reward. Maybe they simply want to outdo their co-workers. Maybe they want to beat their personal best. Whatever the case, if a person feels as if they have something to work towards, they will be motivated to step into the office each day.

In the last section, we discussed the importance of having apparent and measureable goals for your employees, but how do you make those goals accessible and realistic? Without a little bit of guidance, those big-picture goals might seem daunting or too vague to tackle on an individual level. There are several steps you can take to help your employees feel a little more engaged with your company goals.

In chapter six, *No Excuses*, we talked about breaking down your end goals into bite-sized pieces. This is good advice in this chapter as well. Make sure you're going after big goals with little steps. Your team will be able to see the light at the end of the tunnel...even if there are several tunnels to work through. Give them goals they can achieve within the quarter, or even within the month. And then celebrate your victories! Let your employees know you appreciate them. You don't have to throw a party every month, but it doesn't hurt to treat a star performer to lunch or a cup of coffee. Such an action also has the added benefit of a little more one-on-one time with that particular employee—something that can never hurt.

In addition to breaking down your lofty, long-term goals, it is important to use your best resource: your people. If you are leading a marketing team, for example, get them together once a month or once a week and talk about what's going well and what is not. By sharing experiences and swapping stories, your team will help each other grow. If someone did particularly well last month, call on that individual to share what marketing strategies are working well and what strategies are ineffective. On the flip side, coax other "middle-of-the-road" team members to talk by pointing out what they did well last month and asking them about it. They are

> "Motivation is the art of getting people to do what you want them to do because they want to do it."
>
> —Dwight D. Eisenhower

most likely well aware of their short-comings, so pointing them out in front of everyone will do nothing to further motivate them and will only cause undue embarrassment. Instead, say something like, "Roger, I noticed that you did an outstanding job reaching the ages fifty to sixty-five demographic last month. Can you tell us what strategies you used to access that age group?"

You could have just as easily said, "Roger, you missed the mark marketing to young adults last month. What can you do better?" Instead, you've used a little tact and now Roger is sharing his secrets for marketing to middle-aged adults. Not only is the rest of the team reaping the benefits of Roger's knowledge, Roger is also gaining confidence in his abilities *and* is pleased to have a little recognition. Win-win-win.

Another effective way to build skills and motivate employees is through mentoring programs. I have found that when a person takes on a mentoring role, they become more engaged in their work and try hard to ditch their bad habits (at least in front of their mentee!). If you assign someone to mentor a new employee or intern, you are also paying them a huge compliment. You are essentially saying, "I have enough faith in your abilities and teaching prowess to entrust you with a highly impressionable new employee. I hope they will turn out to be just as skilled as you." Pretty high praise, but it's true.

A mentor is someone whom you trust and someone who performs. Of course, you'll want to have a conversation with someone first before you unexpectedly assign them a mentee. When you have that conversation, make your admiration for their abilities apparent. Let them know that they have been carefully selected to fill this role and that you think the new employee or intern would benefit tremendously from their help. Also, be sure to let them know this is not a permanent role (unless they want it to be!). Sometimes people shy away from mentoring because they are leery of the time commitment. If that is a limiting factor, have an open discussion about how much time they can realistically commit to training the green individual.

I am a personal fan of mentoring because it allows me to explain things to others that I am not usually forced to put into words. By talking about a certain concept, I end up finding out what I know about it and what I may need to brush up on. It's hard to know exactly what you know about a topic until you starting explaining it to others.

How About You?

We've spent quite a bit of time talking about building up others' loyalty, but what about your own? You are also, of course, an important part of your organization and it is crucial that you feel steadfast to your company when you are trying to instill a sense of loyalty in others. How can your employees feel committed to your company's mission when you don't share that same loyalty? You might be able to fake it for a while, but in the end, people will be able to see through the façade.

So, how do you build up your own sense of loyalty in your company? Perhaps you don't have an excellent leader like yourself who is reaching out to you, motivating you, and demonstrating that they *actually* give a damn that you come into work every day and work your heart out. Hopefully you do have someone (or several someones) that monitor your work and care about what you do, but I am well aware that this isn't always the case. In such an environment, it is up to you to be your own cheerleader. **It is up to you to build personal loyalty**.

One of the ways to feel proud of the work you do is to use your skills to their fullest extent. Take on projects that give you a healthy challenge. Volunteer for extra assignments that will both use your skill set and provide you with the opportunity to grow. For instance, if you're good at excel spreadsheets and creating systems, volunteer to craft a tracking system for employee improvement next quarter. If you are an excellent writer, volunteer to start a company newsletter. If you are an excellent teacher, volunteer to take on a mentoring position.

There are lots of possibilities if you look for them! Think outside the box and you'll probably come up with a way to make better use of your skill set. In the end, if you find yourself with a full (but not *too* full) docket of somewhat challenging tasks to perform, you'll save yourself from boredom and feel a nip of motivation. Besides, you have a valuable skill set and the motivation to improve yourself (you're reading this book, aren't you?). Why not do everything in your power to use those attributes?

Additionally, don't forget about goal-setting. It's a good idea for the people you lead; it's a good idea for you. Having something in front of you—something that you're constantly working towards—is one of the most important motivators of all. Set your sights on a specific goal (and several smaller goals along the way), work up a sweat, and don't forget to celebrate your accomplishments. You'll end up feeling great about the work you're doing and loyalty will come naturally.

Finally, make sure you strike a balance. If you find yourself working from dawn to dusk, you'll burn out. Working endless hours at the office is not sustainable and can lead to a profound dissatisfaction or resentment of your job. If you feel like your life is being sucked away by work, you're in a dangerous position. Stop. Evaluate. Create a plan to bring a little more balance to your life. Maybe that means turning down a few assignments or leaving the office early on Wednesdays to spend extra time with your daughter. Maybe that means running to the gym for an hour after work. Whatever the case, don't ignore your life outside the office. A person performs at their best when they are feeling healthy and balanced in all aspects of their life. This kind of person does not dread going into the office because they know it is just a slice of their life—an important slice, yes, but a slice none-theless. When you practice this kind of balance, it is much easier to be a loyal, dedicated employee.

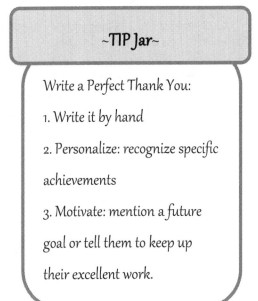

~TIP Jar~

Write a Perfect Thank You:

1. Write it by hand

2. Personalize: recognize specific achievements

3. Motivate: mention a future goal or tell them to keep up their excellent work.

Your arsenal

☑ Start paying attention! Develop a system for keeping track of employee information—both work-related and personal tidbits.

☑ How can you recognize your top performers this quarter? This week? Brainstorm some ideas that will award or identify achievements.

☑ Hold a meeting next week that focuses on strategy and idea-generating. Open the floor to all participants and encourage everyone to share ideas or stories about how they were able to accomplish their goals last quarter. If it is not in your power to hold a meeting, suggest the idea to someone who can.

☑ Does the office have a new employee? Solicit the help of a veteran to give them a little advice, job training, and job shadowing. Check in with both the mentor and mentee from time to time to gauge progress and satisfaction.

☑ Are all your skills being put to use? Jot down a few ideas on how to incorporate more of your expertise in the workplace.

Notes

_____

_____

_____

_____

_____

_____

_____

_____

_____

_____

_____

_____

_____

_____

_____

_____

_____

_____

_____

9. Self-Confidence
Shoulders Back, Head Up.

> "Make the most of yourself,
> for that is all there is of you."
> -Ralph Waldo
> Emerson

My Story

There's a story I often tell in my self-promotion workshop about a figure called "Silent Sally." Before I learned to master my self-perception and confidence, Silent Sally would say to me, "Just sit in the back. Nobody wants to hear what you have to say." And so I disengaged, and that was a terrible thing to do. It wasn't until I identified and eradicated my self-sabotaging tendencies that I began to make a real place for myself at the table. Each and every one of you has your own self-saboteur lurking inside of you and whispering discouraging thoughts in your ear. This chapter is about defeating this self-doubt and reaping the benefits of practiced self-confidence.

Striking a balance between self-assuredness and humility is a constant challenge when you're leading others. It's easy to lose sight of your true values in day-to-day life. Do you have the ability to rise to a challenge or deal with a setback without losing your sense of self? Focus on things like finding the positive in the negative and feeling good about what you've accomplished, and you'll find that your confidence will get a boost and you'll feel better equipped to overcome larger challenges. Now, if only these mindsets were as easy to achieve as they sound!

D.I.Y Confidence

When building self-confidence, we can look to those around us for guidance. You may have observed the way that others with high self-confidence do not depend on obtaining rewards as a confirmation of their success. They are confident in their assertions and aren't afraid to let themselves be heard. Instead of looking to others for recognition, focus on your inner awareness of and belief in your capabilities and past successes.

Pushing yourself to focus on your own previous achievements and skills will enable you to succeed in the future. You've heard it before: Success breeds success. It's a cliché because it's true. Self-confidence is a success enabler.

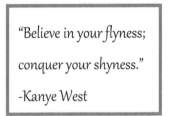

"Believe in your flyness; conquer your shyness."

-Kanye West

When you carry yourself with an air of self-assurance, you're not as likely to be challenged and the people surrounding you—both inside and outside of work—are more prone to believe in you and support your endeavors. **It's often surprising to realize how great an impact the way you think about yourself has on your life**. And that's the thing about confidence: you know you need it, you see the benefit it has for others, but the more you consider it, the more daunted you may feel. This is because considering a thing and actually achieving it are two completely different tasks. And, it probably doesn't help that self-confidence and success may appear effortless for others.

There are several actions you can take in order to promote improved feelings of self-confidence. As I stated earlier, success breeds success. You're probably thinking, "Well great, so how's that supposed to help me? How am I supposed to achieve my 'first win?'" Here's the secret: You already have. Remember that the issue of self-confidence is an issue of self-perception. By this, I mean that if you don't begin to improve your ability to acknowledge your own successes and efforts, it won't matter whether you pay the bills, sign on a new client, or give a successful presentation, let alone solve world hunger. The issue centers on self-awareness and self-appreciation. An important step to developing the ability to pat one's self on the back is to recognize and reject the compulsion to be appreciated and acknowledged by others as a measurement of success in work and life.

It may seem unnatural at first, but consider scheduling a moment to appreciate the hard work that you take for granted. Allotting time to congratulate yourself will help to build your sense of accomplishment and self-worth. And then thank, out loud or to yourself, the source of your accomplishments. Boasting and bragging are inappropriate, but having a clear understanding of your contributions to a particular victory is.

I've observed that women in particular often fall prey to the need for others' affirmations. In today's society, it seems as though women are practically unable to accept any self-congratulations until another has acknowledged their contribution. I see this need less frequently in men, who have often been raised to more immediately perceive their endeavors as successes. Developing this skill, especially for the female professional, is paramount to long-term success and happiness.

All The World's a Stage

So you've recognized your successes and patted yourself on the back—now what? From what you wear to when you speak to the smile on your face, you've got to convince those around you that you believe in yourself and that you've got confidence in your acumen and ability. It's been proven time and time again that **people with low self-esteem subconsciously undermine their own success**; they hold themselves back. This is absolutely true.

As I explained in my opening story, we all have a "self-saboteur" to defeat. This is that voice in the back of your mind constantly causing you to doubt your actions, beliefs, and goals. If we give in to our self-saboteur, we begin to ruin our own opportunities as our self-doubt overtakes our intentions and hopes.

> ~TIP Jar~
>
> Dress for success! Others will take you more seriously if your clothing is clean, wrinkle-free, conservative, and well-fitted. For an added dose of confidence, dress in the "power colors" red and black.

Instead of relaying our message in the calm and collected manner that we know ourselves capable of, our interactions with people are veiled in doubt. When you sound unsure of yourself, those around you feel as though there is a certain risk involved in your project. More than this, you're placing the power of perception in other people's eyes. Who's more likely to achieve the raise at work: the person that enters an office with their head held high, exuding a strong sense of confidence as they state exactly why they deserve a raise OR the hunched-over person that prefaces his or her request with, "Well, now, I know that things have been tight around here lately and that we've even been letting people go, but...?" If you make a real effort to come off as more confident you'll soon realize that you may even begin to convince yourself of your own worth and skills (finally!).

There are several communication studies books written about body language and vocal inflection that emphasize the importance of how we hold ourselves and how we sound. Human beings perceive confidence (and its antithesis: weakness) in a nearly universal way. When we see someone with their shoulders back, their chin up, and a steady gaze, we see confidence. Conversely, when we notice someone fidgeting with their hands in their pockets and a downward or sporadic gaze, we see weakness or nervousness or even someone who is untrustworthy. Think about your body language at your next meeting. Do you tend to cross your arms? Crossing your arms subconsciously sends the message that you are closed off from the rest of the group and that you are forming a protective shell around your body. Do you tend to slouch in your chair during your meetings? Remember to sit up. Good posture shows fearlessness and a willingness to put yourself out there.

And don't forget to smile. Clearly, you don't want to smile too much or smile at inappropriate times (people will wonder what you're up to!), but you do want to come across as a pleasant and approachable individual. Wear a natural smile that says, "I'm relaxed, I'm open, and I have nothing to hide." You'll be amazed by the difference a little positive body language can make. Another benefit: I've read that a smile makes you look ten pounds lighter and five years younger. Who doesn't want that?

The Questions of Confidence

So, you've observed others who exude confidence. You've begun to modify your body language and actions so that you appear more confident. Now it's time to trust yourself and have the courage to make yourself heard. It's time to ask questions.

You're probably wondering how asking questions could possibly make you seem confident in your knowledge and skills, but it's true. I realized many years ago that you're remembered more for the questions you ask than the answers you give. Using this knowledge to your benefit is easy when you apply my "Rule of Three Questions." Simply put, be prepared to walk into every single meeting and ask three questions that demonstrate the following:

1. **Competency**: Your first question should demonstrate that you understand the content of the topic, or that you need more information in order to clearly understand and be able to support it.

2. **Support**: The aim of your second question is to demonstrate support for the presenter or for the material that is being discussed.

3. **Inclusivity**: The final and most important question must be one that demonstrates inclusionary behavior, which I believe to be one of the most necessary components of a successful leadership model.

First of all, show your ***competency*** by making a statement and following it up with a clarifying question. This will demonstrate that you have a good grasp of the topic, but are interested in the nitty-gritty details. For example, "I know we've talked about expanding our sales demographic to a younger, more tech-savvy audience in the upper Midwest. But have we considered the differences in how a male consumer might perceive our new marketing campaign as opposed to a female consumer?" Through this question, you've shown you know your stuff, but are interested in learning more and becoming more deeply involved with the project.

Similarly, you can show your ***support*** for an initiative by making a statement followed by a question. Be careful not to be over-the-top with your praise. Say something like, "I think it's a great idea to change the packaging of our products so that they use fifteen percent less plastic. Our audience should respond well to our 'going green' initiative. But have we thought about how we're going to rework the logo to fit the redesigned packaging?"

Lastly, how can you ask a question that demonstrates *inclusionary* behavior? This process begins by simply taking a look around you. During meetings there are always people in the room whose body language conveys their timidity, confusion, or inability to get their voice heard. The next time you witness someone falling through the conversation cracks, say something such as, "Joe, you look like you're really thinking hard about this. Would you like to share what's on your mind?" Another routinely overlooked group of participants is found tucked inside your meeting's conference call mechanism. It's as simple as asking, "Are there any people out in cyberspace that have a comment or question they'd like to contribute?" Gestures like these open the door to a more open and inclusive dialogue.

Remember that a meeting is not the time to demonstrate the extent of your experience and knowledge. You were invited to the meeting because others believe you have valuable information to share. This is why they want you there. They're interested in the way that you can apply your knowledge to the meeting's agenda. **Prove others right by anticipating what your specific contribution will be**. This way, you'll make your mark in a manner that doesn't detract from the goals of the meeting or override someone else's voice. Demonstrating your willingness to be a person that's not always in the driver's seat—a person who has the confidence to share time at the podium—speaks positively to your character as a professional and a businessperson.

In addition to tactfully encouraging the interaction of others, it's also important to understand how to make others feel comfortable enough not to share too much. There were not only times when I pushed others forward, there were also times when

I had to remind others that they didn't need to tell us everything they knew.

This potentially touchy situation can be dealt with tactfully by relaying your own confidence in the particular team member's intelligence and competence. By building others up, you're often avoiding the compulsion for them to dogmatically parade their knowledge, which typically results from their own anxiety that superiors aren't aware of their worth. When building up others, aim to relay to them that they're needed to help other people with the information and details that they're *most effective at providing*. Figure out where others shine and let them know that you would be interested in hearing their input when that specific topic is brought up at your next meeting. Almost everyone has an area of expertise where they excel; **a great leader cares enough to take the time to identify others' talents and utilize them for the sake of their company's success.**

Confidence in the Face of Criticism

What if someone makes a comment or does something that makes you feel inferior? Despite the cause, how do you rebuild your self-confidence? There's no doubt that each of us has, and will continue to experience, the bite of condescension or belittlement. It can be difficult to believe, but this experience almost always transpires as a result of others feeling threatened by you. It's their method of building their own self-confidence—by making you look or feel inferior. You probably didn't actually say something that was inappropriate, incorrect, or completely off-base. But, even if you did ask a question that was totally outlandish, there are many ways to defuse and defeat the temporary confidence killer.

Compensate for a snafu by saying simply, "Well, out-of-the-box thinking is something that challenges the status quo," or "We may just be thinking differently." Always generate a way to defend what you've said in a positive manner. And remember that humor can also play a fantastic role in emotionally-charged scenarios. **Never be afraid to laugh at yourself!** Another option is to respond to the criticism with a question. Ask the person, "What is it about what I just said that's bothering you?" or "What is it about the idea that isn't valid?" The catch to effectively delivering these questions lies in your ability to be non-confrontational and humble. Be prepared to reestablish understanding—not to fight back. Be calm and do not threaten. A good way to monitor your neutrality index is to pay attention to the tension you're holding in your hands under the table. Are your fingers tensed into a fist or spread open in a non-threatening manner?

> "A successful person is one who can lay a firm foundation with the bricks that others throw at him or her."
>
> -David Brinkley

Having greater self-awareness will strengthen your self-confidence. **The self-aware person already knows where their skills lie and where their greatest contributions can be made**. They're cognizant of the attributes they offer and the position they occupy—not position in the narrow-minded sense of a formal title—but the position of knowledge, wisdom, relationships, and experiences a person offers. Regardless of your height on the company totem pole, you can still offer the experience that people seek in a decision-making process. In the end, self-confidence comes down to self-awareness and the ability to apply and believe in your own voice and particular set of skills. Know what it is that makes your contribution unique and capitalize on it.

The greatest benefit of building self-confidence is the way it enables you to rise above the individual and think in terms of the larger picture. Once you've freed your mind of unnecessary insecurities, you'll finally be able to develop as a leader. This is because, as a leader, it's your responsibility to identify the gifts of those around you, thereby giving those individuals the opportunity to demonstrate their self-confidence by bringing them into a project, proposal, or presentation. When developed and applied in a positive way, self-confidence becomes something that not only lifts you up, but enables you to lift others up as well.

Your arsenal

- ☑ At your next meeting, practice asking the "three question types."

- ☑ Take time to examine your self-perception. What are you doing that might undermine your self-confidence? What steps can you take to correct these habits?

- ☑ Set aside time to recognize your successes. Reward your progress!

- ☑ Practice acting! When you walk into a room or encounter someone new, make sure your shoulders are up, your head is held high, and there's a smile on your face.

- ☑ Two times a day, speak up. Practice asserting your opinions in a friendly, but confident way.

- ☑ Focus on inclusionary behavior. What can you do to lift others up and let their voices be heard?

Notes

10. Building Community

Be open. Connect with others.

> "Life's most persistent and urgent question is, 'What are you doing for others?'"
>
> -Martin Luther King Junior

My Story

Nearly everyone longs to be a part of something bigger than they are—to be a part of a community that cares about their well-being, success, and psyche. It is natural (and healthy) to reach out to others and attempt to form group bonds. This tendency is of utmost importance at work, where your relationships with others could help advance your career or drag you down. Therefore, it is quite unsettling when others attempt to interfere with your community-building.

I was once approached by a colleague with a very unexpected and uncomfortable suggestion: he thought I should distance myself from a particular co-worker and went as far as to suggest that by associating with this other female colleague, I was actually hurting my career.

I *believe* that this man was speaking from a place of genuine interest in my well-being—he *thought* he was doing me a favor. I knew that the person with which he wanted me to stop associating had, as of late, lost some of upper management's support. However, I perceived this recent lack of support to be due to misunderstanding, not due to a lack of skills or business acumen. I found this person to be extremely intelligent and was learning a lot from her. So, as much as she was a personal friend, she was also someone who was teaching and guiding me with her experience and education.

Instead of accepting my colleague's advice, I decided to respond by sharing the positive things about my relationship with this particular female co-worker. I described what I learned and valued as a result of associating with her and attempted to show a side of this person to him that he did not know. I asked him, "What better choice than to befriend someone who challenges my thinking and exposes me to things that she has learned and experienced that I have not?"

I'm sharing this story to demonstrate just how complicated the nature of a community can be. There will be (and surely have been) times when a co-worker approaches you, just like the colleague who entered my office that day, and attempts to sabotage your relationship with someone—your community. Each day we're confronted with challenges, whether self-created or created by others, that make us want to draw a line in the sand, exclude someone, or burn bridges and cut ties (not to mention all of the larger social ideologies that our worlds contain that seem to label and limit us!). However, this chapter is not about the chaos that attempts to pull us apart. Instead, this chapter is about building a community that flourishes and benefits its members through reciprocity, respect, and courageous leadership.

What is a Community?

Consider your average work day. How many people do you pass on your way to a meeting or on your way to the coffee machine? How many of those people do you greet or acknowledge? It can be shocking to realize that we could work the entire day without any real human interaction. You might make dozens of phone calls, shoot off sixty emails, and send a handful of text messages, but how many face-to-face conversations do you have on an average day at the office? How many people do you pass regularly that you do not know or know very little about? Based on your answer to these questions, how would you classify your sense of community at work?

It's not always an easy task to build relationships. Reaching out to people can mean stepping outside of your comfort zone. Becoming someone's advocate can be even more of a push. But, despite the extra work, building communities is a necessary part of a successful career and life. The more you expand and foster your connections, the more benefits you'll experience.

So, communities are important. But what are these things, really? There's really no exact answer. This is because they're based on relationships, and we all seek and enjoy different things in our relationships with others. In a broader sense, think of your community as those you know and with whom you consistently come into direct contact, such as neighbors and co-workers. These people are closest to you—not just geographically but also in terms of human intimacy. However, this group does not have to be limited to a select few. **The best community builders**

approach each connection with an equal level of authenticity and a willingness to invite others into their community. If you just think about your community or network as a means to an end, you'll be less effective and miss out on the sustainable benefits.

How To Build Community

~TIP Jar~

Test your listening skills!

Challenge yourself to remember three important details from every conversation you have this week. Jot down those details immediately and then try to recall them two or three hours later. Can you do it?

To be a great networker and community builder you must eschew the typical "race-to-the-top" lens that we often encounter in highly competitive business atmospheres. Make your relationships genuine. If you care about the people you meet and the relationships you establish, then you're building a genuine community instead of a superficial connection. Yes, meeting new people can be an awkward and uncomfortable challenge, but it's worth it. Push past your initial hesitations and go in with the mentality that meeting new people is actually *good*. New people have the power to reenergize, offer fresh perspectives, diversify, and add a little challenge and change to our lives.

Keep in mind that the people you meet through work and your network are not always people with whom you have a lot in common, and these people may not appear to be a natural fit in your community. This can be a hurdle in attempting to connect and you may have to step even farther outside of your comfort zone to make a connection. However, never rule anyone out, and avoid classifying your interactions with people at all costs. Think of each relationship as a potential addition to your community and, despite obvious differences, leave that invitation open. And don't forget to keep an open mind. Even if someone may appear to have nothing in common with you on the surface, dig a little deeper. Human beings have depth and I have often found myself surprised by someone's back story or hobbies or family life. You never know unless you ask.

The trick is asking the right questions *and* showing a genuine interest in the answers. Keep your questions open and noninvasive and chime in with your own anecdotes. If you feel the conversation going deeper, let it. If not, that's ok. A connection has been made and maybe next time they will feel more comfortable about opening up.

Above all, show your co-worker that you genuinely care. Inquire, express interest or concern, share stories, give and receive advice. And don't forget to listen! In our modern, self-centered society, there is a shortage of good listeners. Remember to focus on what your companion is saying before thinking up a reply. It is easy to lose ourselves in our own thoughts and completely gloss over what others are saying. Don't forget to pay attention to body language as well as the words your co-worker is saying. Both can speak volumes.

Advocacy and the Psychological Brand

The authenticity you promote among your community not only benefits those relationships, it also builds what is referred to as your *psychological brand*. People you have never met before are exposed to your brand indirectly. Unlike the *experiential* aspect of your brand—the image you've developed through direct interactions—your psychological brand is promoted through word of mouth. Others develop an impression of you based on what they learn through their network. Perhaps these people have only passed you in the hallway. Even so, they've been exposed to your psychological brand.

The extensive reach of your psychological brand is one of the benefits of network and community development. The best way to harness this power is to ensure that your interactions with others are always positive. This way, the psychological aspect of your brand is always working *for* you, not *against* you. Safeguard your positive image by remaining aware of the way you contribute to your interactions. Before meeting with someone, resolve to make what I refer to as an "energy deposit" instead of an "energy withdrawal." Every person you come into contact with should feel positive and

> "I alone cannot change the world, but I can cast a stone across the waters to create many ripples."
>
> -Mother Teresa

energized after their encounter with you. Don't overwhelm others with stress or negativity that leaves them feeling exhausted and overwhelmed. Instead, make them feel a sense of calm and relief from your interaction.

And don't forget to carry that positivity with you even when you think others aren't watching. Today, we have the added concern of our social media or digital presence. A negative tweet or derogatory Facebook comment can have more power than you think. If one of your co-workers finds out that you are griping about company policies online, how do you think that looks? Even if you are making comments in jest, don't be certain that others will get the joke. In short, **practice keeping it positive *at all times*.** That way, others will begin to count on your consistently optimistic attitude and will know they can rely on you to be level-headed and encouraging when a difficult situation arises. Your co-workers are likely to value your positive psychological brand and recognize you as an indispensible component of the office community.

The power of a positive psychological brand revealed itself to me early in my career in the form of a big break (additionally, I learned at the same time that advocacy comes from the most unexpected places). It all began roughly twenty-five years ago when someone that I had never considered to be a professional connection blindsided me with a fantastic opportunity to advance my career within my current organization. This unexpected advocacy came to me as a surprise because I had never worked closely with this individual—our relationship had always been informal and distant. I now realize that it was my success at creating a positive psychological brand image in my community that caused this person to reach out to me. Had there been some doubt or worry surrounding my brand—had something stuck out negatively—this individual would not have gone out of his way to add me to the list of candidates vying for the position. But, because my interactions with this individual's extended network had been wholly positive, and he had considered my attitude a valuable asset, I was given the opportunity to take on a job that expanded my community, network, and responsibility. With this new position came plenty of changes, challenges, and accountability, as well as excellent opportunities for personal growth. Although my stature within the company changed dramatically, I was always careful to remember what got me there in the first place—positive, energy-filled interactions and an unwavering commitment to reach out and engage my community of co-workers.

Your Contribution

You become a true member of a community when it sees you as someone of value. This doesn't mean that you have to be the leader, part the sea, or make them all rich—but you must play an active role that is consistent with the way you want people to think about you. What role do you want to play and what image do you want to create for yourself? Are you Maggie in Marketing who brings great treats? Or Margaret Inc., who's recognized as a business professional, a strong idea-generator, and influencer? Which would you prefer? If you're comfortable being recognized as Maggie in Marketing who brings delicious treats and makes great conversation, then go for it—bring the best damn treats you can. But, if that's not what you want to be, then stop!

Envision what you'd like to be and where you'd like to go in one year. Five years. Dream big and make a realistic plan to get there. Remember, your biggest obstacle in achieving your aspirations is YOU. Don't let your mental inhibitions get in the way of doing exactly what you—Maggie in Marketing or Margaret Inc.—wants to do. By constantly reaching upward and bettering yourself, you are also bettering the community around you. Others will benefit from your ambition, drive, and willingness to contribute. And remember to lean on your community when you need to (you can't excel at *everything* after all) and, in return, let them lean on you. Figuring out your niche within your workplace community and striving to be the best you can be within that role is a huge part of building trust and rapport amongst co-workers. Making a meaningful contribution to your work community builds others' confidence in your abilities and skills *and* can strengthen your chances for achieving your goals.

So, prove yourself! Start today. Even if you're not currently fulfilling your dream role within your organization, do whatever tasks you are assigned with your head held high and a positive mind frame. Think, "I will do my job and I will do it well." Let that be your mantra as you keep your eye on your long-term goals and aspirations. Believe me, others will take notice.

Keep in mind that your community (like yourself) is what you make it. If you make the resolution to start developing your brand differently or to reshape your contribution to your community, you'll begin to notice the benefits in your career. Enter into each social scenario with the intention of being authentic, inclusive, and making an energy deposit and you're sure to start discovering your own advocates in unexpected places, not to mention a handful of others whose lives you'll change with your own advocacy.

What can you do today to contribute to your community?

Your arsenal

☑ Make a point of saying hello to anyone you encounter in the office today. Address them by their name when you greet them.

☑ Think about your co-workers. Who might challenge you and help you the most in your career? Make a point to build that person (or people) into your community, but don't force it or fake it! This is about learning, not about brown-nosing.

☑ Instead of sending an email to your co-worker down the hall today, walk to their office and have a brief chat instead.

☑ Get out of your comfort zone! Attend a networking or other social event this month and make as many meaningful connections as you can.

☑ Think about how you want to be recognized in your office community. What are your short-term and long-term goals? Jot out a plan to get there.

Notes

_____

_____

_____

_____

_____

_____

_____

_____

_____

_____

_____

_____

_____

_____

_____

_____

_____

_____

Afterward

Here's to you!

You've periodically taken ten minutes of your time to discover the leader you know you are. I am grateful for the time you spent with me and look forward to future encounters.

My hope is that you have realized that no one has the title of leader on their business card or on the name plate outside of their office. It's who you are and how you "play" in this world that gives you that designation. Everyone has the opportunity to lead.

YOU have the potential to create a new reality of leadership or in the words of Rumi, a 13th century poet:

You were born with potential.
You were born with goodness and trust.
You were born with ideals and dreams.
You were born with greatness.
You were born with wings.
You were not meant for crawling, so don't.
You have wings.
Learn to use them and fly.

Here's to the Leader within...

Respectfully Studied
Thank you for your insight.

Much of this book is written from my personal experiences, but another large portion was inspired by the writings and insights of other business leaders. Here is a list of books and articles I referred to while writing *The 10-Minute Leadership Challenge*. I highly recommend adding these titles to your summer reading list.

-Margaret

Chapter 1: Authenticity

Goffee, Rob and Gareth Jones. "Managing Authenticity: The Paradox of Great Leadership." *Harvard Business Review*, December, 2005. http://hbr.org/2005/12/managing-authenticity-the-paradox-of-great-leadership/ar/1

Guignon, Charles. *On Being Authentic: Thinking in Action.* New York: Routledge, 2004.

Lencioni, Patrick. *Getting Naked: A Business Fable about Shedding the Three Fears of Client Loyalty.* San Francisco: Jossey-Bass, 2010.

Rosenbloom, Stephanie. "For Only The Authentic," *New York Times*, September 9, 2011.
http://www.nytimes.com/2011/09/11/fashion/for-only-the-

authentic-cultural-studies.html

Wright, Karen. "Dare to Be Yourself." *Psychology Today*, May 1, 2008. http://www.psychologytoday.com/articles/200804/dare-be-yourself

Chapter 2: Courage

Alexander, Rebecca. "Performing under pressure: How to think on your feet." *Management Today*. July 1, 2011. http://www.managementtoday.co.uk/features/1076944/Performing-pressure-think-feet/

Brown, Brene. *Daring Greatly: How the Courage to be Vulnerable Transforms the Way We Live.* New York, NY: Gotham Books, 2012.

Martin, Iain C. *Worthy of Their Esteem: The Timeless Words and Sage Advice of Abraham Lincoln.* Kennebunkport, ME: Cider Mill Press, 2009.

Nepo, Mark. *Finding Inner Courage*. San Francisco, CA: Conari Press, 2007.

Sherman, Josepha. *Jeff Bezos: King of Amazon*. Kirkland, WA: 21st Century, 2001.

Chapter 3: Trust

Collingwood, Jane. "Trust and Vulnerability in Relationships," *Psych Central*, last modified March 27, 2013.

http://psychcentral.com/lib/2008/trust-and-vulnerability-in-relationships/

Covey, Stephen. *The Speed of Trust: The One Thing That Changes Everything.* New York: Free Press, 2008.

Hawley, Katherine. *Trust: A Very Short Introduction.* Oxford, UK: Oxford University Press, 2012.

Levering, Robert and Milton Moskowitz. "100 Best Companies to Work For." *CNN Money.* 2013. http://money.cnn.com/magazines/ fortune/best-companies/?iid=bc_lp_header.

Martinuzzi, Bruna, "The Power of Trust: A Steel Cable," *Mind Tools*, 2009, accessed March 27, 2013. http://www.mindtools.com/pages/article/newLDR_46.htm

Saleem, Hasan. "How to Delegate Effectively." Directory Journal. June 23, 2007. www.dirjournal.com.

Solomon, Robert C., and Fernando Flores. *Building Trust: In Business, Politics, Relationships, and Life.* New York, NY: Oxford University Press, 2001.

Chapter 4: Being Present

Barker, Eric. "The Biggest Difference Between Happiness and Meaningfulness," *Business Insider* Blog, January 16, 2013. http://www.businessinsider.com/what-does-it-take-to-have-a-happy- and-meaningful-life-2013-1

Brown, Kirk Warren; Ryan, Richard M. "The benefits of being present: Mindfulness and its role in psychological well-being," *Journal of Personality and Social Psychology* 84(4) (2003): 822-848.

Creagan, Edward T., M.D. "Dispatch distractions by living in the moment." *Mayo Clinic Stress Blog,* September 26, 2012. http://www.mayoclinic.com/health/stress-and-distraction/MY02240

Formica, Michael J. "5 Steps for Being Present." *Psychology Today,* June 14, 2011. http://www.psychologytoday.com/blog/enlightened-living/201106/5-steps-being-present

Schwartz, Tony. "The Energy Project." www.tonyschwartz.com/blog.

Zander, Rosamund Stone, and Benjamin Zander. *The Art Of Possibility: Transforming Professional   and Personal Life.* Boston: Harvard Business School Press, 2002.

Chapter 5: Balancing Heart/Head

Bryant, John Hope. *Love Leadership: The New Way to Lead in a Fear-Based World.* San Francisco, CA: Jossey-Bass, 2009.

Cashman, Kevin. *Leadership from the Inside Out: Seven Pathways to Mastery.* Provo, UT: Executive Excellence Publishing, 1998.

Kelly, Matthew. "My Spiritual Journey." Beacon Publishing, 2012. CD.

Tan, Chade-Meng. (2010, November 11) TED Talks: Everyday Compassion at Google. http://www.ted.com/talks/chade_meng_tan_everyday_compassi on_at_google.html

Williams, Ray. *Breaking Bad Habits: The Science of Habit Management.* Amazon Digital Services, Inc., 2011.

Chapter 6: No Excuses

Charan, Ram. *Leadership in the Era of Economic Uncertainty*. New York: McGraw-Hill, 2008.

Pascal, Dennis. *Getting the Right Things Done: A Leader's Guide to Planning and Execution*. Cambridge, MA: Lean Enterprise Institute, 2006.

Mayo Clinic, "When and how to say no," *Mayo Clinic*, last modified July 23, 2010, http://www.mayoclinic.com/health/stress-relief/SR00039

Useem, Michael. The Go Point: When It's Time to Decide— Knowing What to Do and When to Do It. New York:Crown Business, 2009.

Zadra, Dan. *Where will you be five years from today?* Seattle:

Compendium, Inc., 2009.

Chapter 7: Clarity

Miller, Blake. "The Importance of a Mission Statement," *Think Big Partners*, December 9, 2010.
http://www.thinkbigpartners.com/start-a-business/202-the-importance-of-a-mission-statement.html

Boundless. "The Importance of Clarity in Professional Settings."
https://www.boundless.com/business/business-writing/introduction-to-business-communications/importance-clarity-in-professional-settings/

Harvard Business Essentials: Business Communication. Boston: Harvard Business School Press, 2003.

Myhre Hayes, Susan. *Peace in the Puzzle: Becoming Your Intended Self.* Minneapolis: MyhreHayesGroup, 2011.

Seidler, Margaret. *Power Surge: A Conduit for Enlightened Leadership.* Amherst, MA: HRD Press, 2010.

Chapter 8: Demonstrating Loyalty

Biro, Meghan M., "5 Leadership Behaviors Loyal Employees Trust," *Forbes Magazine,* June 4, 2012,
http://www.forbes.com/sites/meghanbiro/2012/06/04/5-leadership-behaviors-loyal-employees-trust/

Covey, Stephen R. *Principle-Centered Leadership.* New York: Simon and Schuster, 1992.

Kotter, John P. *Leading Change.* Boston: Harvard Business Press, 1996.

Lencioni, Patrick. *The Five Dysfunctions of a Team.* San Francisco: Jossey-Bass, 2002.

Reichheld, Frekerick F. *The Loyalty Effect: The Hidden Force Behind Growth, Profits, and Lasting Value.* Boston: Harvard Business Press, 1996.

Chapter 9: Self-Confidence

Cain, Susan. *Quiet: The Power of Introverts in a World That Can't Stop Talking.* New York: Crown Business, 2012.

Klaus, Peggy. *Brag! The Art of Tooting Your Own Horn Without Blowing It.* New York: Warner Business Books, 2004.

Kuschner, Harold. *Overcoming Life's Disappointments.* Harpswell, ME: Anchor Publishing, 2007.

Seus Geisel, Dr. Theodor. *Oh the Places You'll Go!* New York: Random House, 1990.

Tannen, Deborah . *Talking 9 to 5: Men and Women at Work.* New York: William Morrow Paperbacks, 1995.

Chapter 10: Community

Kelley, Tom. *The Ten Faces of Innovation: IDEO's Strategies for Defeating the Devil's Advocate and Driving Creativity Throughout Your Organization*. New York: Currency/Doubleday, 2005.

Keltner, Dacher, Marsh, Jason and Jeremy Adam Smith, eds., *The Compassion Instinct*. New York: W.W. Norton & Company, 2010.

Manning, George, Curtis, Kent and Steve McMillen. *Building Community: The Human Side of Work*. Duluth: Whole Person Associates, Inc., 1996.

Rajkumar, Roshini. *Communicate That! Your Toolbox for Powerful Presentations*. Andover, MN: Roshini Multi Media, Inc., 2010.

Wickelgren, Ingrid, "The Importance of Being Social," *The Scientific American*, April 24, 2012, http://blogs.scientificamerican.com/streams-of-consciousness/2012/04/24/the-importance-of-being-social/

Connect
Bring *The 10-Minute Leadership Challenge* to Life

Book a Workshop or Presentation with Margaret Smith for your entire workplace. Here are some of the available workshops, which can be catered to fit your organization's needs:

- ✓ The 10-Minute Leadership Challenge
- ✓ No Fail Networking
- ✓ 10 Secrets to a Lasting Impression
- ✓ 7 Seconds to Success
- ✓ Your Leadership Brand
- ✓ Insights Discovery® Workshop

Margaret Smith also offers one-on-one coaching. Connect with her and find out how *you* can implement strategies from *The 10-Minute Leadership Challenge*.

Find Margaret on:

Twitter: @YouExcelNow
LinkedIn: www.linkedin.com/in/margaretsmithuxl
Facebook: www.facebook.com/uxlnow

For more information on workshops and one-on-one coaching, please visit the UXL website or send a direct message to Margaret Smith:

www.YouExcelNow.com
Margaret@YouExcelNow.com

Margaret B. Smith is the founder of UXL, a career coaching firm specializing in personal and professional development. She spent many years in corporate business leadership positions, works with several non-profit organizations, and teaches at a local university. Learn more about Margaret and contact her through her website: www.YouExcelNow.com

Made in the USA
Charleston, SC
10 December 2013